Edinburgh, M

C000019105

20 00079226 5808

£2.99

13

## Stress Fractures: Essays on Poetry

*Edited by* Tom Chivers

Tom Chivers was born in South London in 1983. He is Director of Penned in the Margins and Co-Director of London Word Festival. His debut collection *How To Build A City* (Salt Publishing, 2009) was shortlisted for the London New Poets Award and his pamphlet *The Terrors* (Nine Arches Press, 2009) for the Michael Marks Award. He edited the anthologies *Generation Txt* (2006) and *City State: New London Poetry* (2009). A regular reviewer for *Poetry London*, in October 2009 he presented a documentary about the poet Barry MacSweeney for BBC Radio 4.

# Stress Fractures
## Essays on Poetry

*Edited by* Tom Chivers

Penned in the Margins
LONDON

PUBLISHED BY PENNED IN THE MARGINS
22 Toynbee Studios, 28 Commercial Street, London E1 6AB
www.pennedinthemargins.co.uk

All rights reserved

Introduction and selection © Tom Chivers
Copyright of the texts rests with the authors

The right of Tom Chivers to be identified as the editor of this work has been asserted by him in accordance with Section 77 of the Copyright, Designs and Patent Act 1988.

This book is in copyright. Subject to statutory exception and to provisions of relevant collective licensing agreements, no reproduction of any part may take place without the written permission of Penned in the Margins.

First published 2010
This edition published 2016


Printed in the United Kingdom by Lightning Source


ISBN
978-0-9565467-1-5

This book is sold subject to the condition that it shall not, by way of trade or otherwise, be lent, re-sold, hired out, or otherwise circulated without the publisher's prior consent in any form of binding or cover other than that in which it is published and without a similar condition including this condition being imposed on the subsequent purchaser.

# CONTENTS

# Stress Fractures

# Introduction

As a kid growing up in South London, one of the highlights of my year was the visit of the Chinese State Circus to Brockwell Park. Into the hilly expanse of green space wedged between the urban neighbourhoods of Brixton, Herne Hill and Norwood would come these lithe, muscled, impossibly exotic entertainers: acrobats, tumblers, strong-men and fire-eaters. The Big Top was a strange, other world, governed by Sun Wukong: the Monkey King. Entry was a contract – for the duration of the show, you agreed to be bound to the rules and internal logic of the tent.

In the final essay in this book, Katy Evans-Bush compares the poetic line to a high-wire act ('the line must be taut, and strong enough to hold'); but poetry is also clowning *and* the taming of the lion. It is circus without the ringmaster.

In *Stress Fractures* I hope to stimulate new conversations about poetry, with all the infelicities of its language (to borrow Ross Sutherland's phrase). The essays are not unified around a particular set of themes, but approach a wide range of subjects. A radically reinterpreted Emily Dickinson mingles with British hip-hop artist Roots Manuva; a teacher's perspective on poetry in education appears alongside investigations into computer-generated writing. Poetry is conceived as a broad ~~church~~ tent which entertains the constant play of contradictory forces *or fractures* (tradition/innovation, private/public, freedom/control); and as an artform stretching, connecting, collaborating and making sense of its new positions in a rapidly-changing cultural landscape.

Much has been written about the decline in space available in mainstream culture for literary criticism in this country; the increasing commercialisation of publishing; and the dispersal of critical culture to the unrestricted – and virtually unrefereeable – territory of the internet.

Some of this is nostalgic grumbling for a golden age that probably never existed in the first place. Much of it certainly overlooks the opportunities to exploit new technologies (the internet, yes, but also digital printing) to generate new dialogue. We are, I believe, witnessing the growth of a tendency towards cultural democratisation, in which the static roles of writer, reader, critic, academic and consumer, as well as the hierarchical structures of publication, distribution and reception that hold those roles in place, are becoming unstable.

In his essay, Theodoros Chiotis responds to this new environment by making the case for a 'multidimensional, interdisciplinary' digital poetics which disrupts the authority of the writer, and stimulates new modes of cognition in the reader. To similar ends, Ross Sutherland shares his own experiments with SYSTRAN translation software to create a collaborative robot poetry. Both envisage a new, dispersed kind of authorship, though one with precursors in, respectively, Modernism and Science Fiction.

I am glad to include Tim Clare's playful deconstruction of Slam Poetry. It seems to me that performance poetry in general has existed for too long without a strong critical culture, and that a certain stream of anti-intellectualism within that broad artform has limited its capacity for innovation. Hannah Silva's work straddles performance poetry, theatre and live arts, and certainly doesn't lack innovation. Her fascinating essay 'Composing Speech' unlocks some of the secrets of her practice as a writer/ performer, such as talking backwards and the peculiarly named art of 'double tonguing'.

Silva's essay contributes to wider conversations about the relationship between poetry and performance, live art and text-based visual art. In 'Radio and...' James Wilkes records an imaginary conversation with

Holly Pester; as regular collaborators, their work explores the poetry of radio transmissions and spoken broadcasts: 'the ruined voice'.

A widely acknowledged association between poetry and hip-hop is developed by David Barnes in his essay on British rapper Roots Manuva, whose lyrics he evaluates in relation to the Romantic poets and Wesleyan theology. Luke Kennard's contribution approaches the fictional space or 'engine room' of the poem via early 20th century comic strips and the music of Nick Cave, David Berman and Smog. And in 'Emily Dickinson, Vampire Slayer', Sophie Mayer investigates the many cultural afterlives of the seminal American writer in visual arts, photography, music, and on YouTube.

That poetry is seen here to intersect with pop culture constitutes neither some desperate plea for 'relevance' nor a nose-dive towards the lowest common denominator; rather, it demonstrates an open, interdisciplinary critical mode which supports a view of poetry in flux with its cultural surroundings. I am keen to reject the notion that poetry and all poets exist in a special bubble, aloof and disconnected.

Emily Critchley focuses her attention on the American writer Lyn Hejinian, a major figure within Language poetry whose activities since the 1970s have been anything but disconnected. She is, for instance, an energetic supporter of cross-genre collaborations between poets and other artists. Critchley's essay carefully unpicks the creative, critical and philosophical dynamics at play within Hejinian's work.

Some of the essays in *Stress Fractures* point towards a new direction in contemporary poetry, a vision that breaks out of the factionalism of the past forty years. Simon Turner identifies a resurgence of interest in Oulipo writing techniques amongst a number of younger British poets, arguing that this could provide a means of combining radical experimentation with the concern for form and craft that characterises mainstream poetry. American writer and critic Adam Fieled, meanwhile, provides an illuminating and necessarily subjective examination of 'post-avant' poetry – a problematic term, but one which has generated new energies on both sides of the Atlantic.

As a literary critic, David Caddy is interested in the social histories of artistic communities: the relationships, shared spaces and chance meetings that underpin creative expression. His essay here is concerned with both the history *and future* of the prose poem in English poetry, characterising it as a 'hybrid form' with the ability to 'absorb a wide range of discourse'.

Caddy's subject is the poem without its most identifiable feature – the line break. Katy Evans-Bush follows with 'The Line', an extensive analysis of the poetic line which draws on examples from Sharon Olds, Basil Bunting, Marianne Moore and others, and which is filtered through a reading of high-wire walker Philippe Petit's *On the High Wire*.

There is much hand-wringing within the arts over the 'relevance' of poetry to children. Indeed, as I write, the Arts Council of England has just made available a major new funding stream to enable poetry organisations to engage with young people. Alex Runchman gives a refreshingly frank assessment of poetry in education from his experiences as a secondary school teacher. He describes a largely conservative educational culture in which poetry is often badly taught and routinely reduced to exam fodder, and argues for a more liberated approach in which poetry can be both studied *and* enjoyed. Specifically, he calls for more poetry to be written for teenagers.

I originally conceived of this book as a kind of almanac – a form suggesting the collection of sundry data, facts, chronologies, and so on.[1] I hope to

---

[1] I was partly inspired by reading Daniel Brine (ed.), *The Live Art Almanac* (London: Live Art Development Agency, 2008).

have maintained something of the miscellany in *Stress Fractures*. This is not an academic publication, though a number of the contributors hold postgraduate degrees, and there are plenty of footnotes to point the diligent reader towards further study. Most of the contributors are themselves poets, and some of the essays will appeal to writers, but this is not a book solely for practitioners. Like the Big Top, anyone is welcome.

The artist Marc Chagall said: 'For me a circus is a magic show that appears and disappears like a world. A circus is disturbing. It is profound.' I hope the essays that follow offer you glimpses into a world that can be both disturbing and profound, but also fun, mischievous and exhilarating.

Tom Chivers
London, September 2010

# THE ARCHITECTURE OF FICTIONAL ROOMS

Interrogating the metaphor: Luke Kennard on secret
rooms, strange endings and early 20th century comics

It's not that students don't "get" Kafka's humour but that we've
taught them to see humour as something you *get* – the same
way we've taught them that a self is something you just *have*.
No wonder they cannot appreciate the really central Kafka joke:
that the horrific struggle to establish a human self results in a self
whose humanity is inseparable from that horrific struggle. That
our endless and impossible journey toward home is in fact our
home. (64-65)

David Foster Wallace, *Consider the Lobster*

People sure love unsolved mysteries, don't they?

Scott Plangenhoef on the music video for Radiohead's 'Just'

As a young child I had the same recurring nightmare about a secret room
behind the gas oven in my gran's kitchen[1] so many times that one day I

---

[1] The room was dark, bigger than the house itself and filled with a reddish light.
There appeared to be what I now recognise as a religious ritual taking place within
it. Although actually I don't recall there being any people. Perhaps the ritual had just
finished.

insisted on moving the oven out with my dad (a man whose preternatural patience on this occasion shaded almost into indulgence) so I could look behind it. I discovered a slightly greasy wall and a gas pipe. I often set novels in this house (as in novels I'm reading), whether the house fits the author's description or not, and I still dream about it – I recently dreamt about chipping the wall away with a pallet knife to find the room was there after all. Faced with incontrovertible evidence that the room doesn't exist I still can't let it go.

My thesis here is that poetry creates a fictional space which itself contains a fictional space; a dream within a dream which acts as a kind of engine room for whatever engaging, mysterious effects the poem has. This is going to involve examples of language and popular culture which could be accused of obfuscation to hide their ultimate emptiness[2], a Russian Doll which is missing its central, solid doll.[3] So I want to suggest that in poetry, as in art in general, one of our most satisfying reactions is 'WTF?', and that there's a good 'WTF?' and a bad 'WTF?' between which every writer must negotiate. I want to start by looking at three songs, which I believe

---

[2] C.f. IMDB comments about any David Lynch movie, the ending of *The Sopranos* or, indeed, any open-ended narrative: the suspicion that the writer/director is just trying to bilk you on a satisfying denouement because they "can't be bothered" to come up with a decent ending or are "taking the piss" out of people who claim ambiguity is intellectually satisfying.

[3] E.g. a kind of Paul Auster self-parody wherein an uninspired writer discovers an unfinished manuscript by an uninspired writer about an uninspired writer discovering an unfinished manuscript... I haven't found them, but I'm pretty certain there are a couple of meta-fictional Mills & Boon novels with a hero/heroine who happens to be an uninspired romantic novelist and whose "real-life" adventures feed into the novel he/she's working on.

manifest directly (or overtly conceal) something necessary to all poetry –
('a poem should resist meaning / almost successfully' - Wallace Stevens)
– 'The Farmer's Hotel' by David Berman of the Silver Jews, 'Fable of the
Brown Ape' by Nick Cave, and Smog's 'Keep Some Steady Friends Around'.
Actually, before that I want to talk about the use of quotation marks in early
20th century comic strips.

George Herriman's *Krazy & Ignatz* concerns the relationship
between Krazy Kat, a naïve, whimsical Kat in love with Ignatz, a mouse who
hates him and has made it his sole *raison d'être* to throw a brick at his head
(a gesture Krazy misinterprets as a declaration of love); and Offissa Pupp, a
police dog committed to protecting Krazy Kat ostensibly to keep the peace,
but actually due to his unrequited love for Krazy and hatred of Ignatz. The
action takes place in the deserts of Coconino County, Arizona. One way or
another, and usually as a result of every plan backfiring at once, Krazy Kat
always gets hit with a brick and Ignatz ends up in jail. Every page-long strip
has the same plot; it ran from 1913 to 1944. The dialogue is widely lauded for
its poetic and eccentric phrasing but, while I concur that it's delightful, it's
not what I want to focus on here. Rather I want to look at Herriman's curious
habit of placing important nouns in speech marks:

DAWGUNNIT, NOW MY "COMEDY" IS RUINED!!! (p. 68)

I WILL NOW SCAN THE "NORTH" – ALL'S WELL THERE. (p. 97)

SHUX, "MOUSE", YOU'RE JUST A AMATEUR HIDER – I'LL SHOW YOU HOW TO
HIDE A "BRICK" SO THAT EVEN THE 103RD EYE WON'T EVER LOCATE IT...
(p. 80)

The speech marks affect the way you sound the line out in your head;

they place a surreal focus on the noun in question and hint at something which isn't really there, acknowledging the falsity (there is no such thing as North in an ink drawing of a dog with a telescope standing on a tower).

## there is no such thing as North in an ink drawing of a dog with a telescope standing on a tower

In any given strip, the things placed within speech marks – whether objects, directions or abstract concepts – are the chess pieces Herriman is going to manoeuvre through the same plot. Although obliviously content with his situation, Krazy Kat's regular song, which concludes several strips over the 31 year run, is "THERE IS A HEPPY LEND FURFUR A-WAAY!!!"

Tony Millionaire's contemporary comic *Maakies*[4] began with the same traditional cartoon theme of eternal recurrence. It's a work of remarkable draftsmanship, harking back to the *Krazy & Ignatz* era in its line-quality, juxtaposed with every extreme of lewdness conceivable. Two sailors, Drinky Crow (a crow) and Uncle Gabby (an ape) are drinking on a boat. They discuss something, perhaps aided by supporting cast; the theme is usually the pointlessness of life or the uncontrollability of our appetites or instincts. Drinky Crow then drinks too much (accompanied by the eminently quotable "Dook-dook-dook-dook-dook!") and shoots himself in the head. The strip is replete with insults and bawdiness which sound at once everyday and horrifyingly oblique:

---

[4] On the meaning of the name: "I can't release that information until a certain person dies... Because he or she would be extremely pissed off to even know that that name was being used." (interview with Millionaire in *The Comics Journal*, 2003).

MAYBE YOU SHOULD CRAWL BACK INSIDE YOUR MOTHER AND TRY AGAIN (p.8)

BULLETS THAT SAY "PENIS" ON THEM!! DON'T JUST KILL!! INSULT!! (p.48)

Speech marks are used more sparingly than in earlier comics – thus stand out all the more. Drifting in a sailboat, Drinky Crow apologises for getting drunk and ruining the day. As it was Drinky Crow's sober self, henceforth referred to as "Sobie", who elected to drink the booze (putting the "kibosh" on their plans for a good sail), Uncle Gabby reasons that they should always be drunk in order to prevent "Sobie" making any more bogus decisions.

HA HA!

exclaims Drinky Crow,

I SEE! WE WILL FOOL "SOBIE" AT HIS OWN GAME!
(Maakies Corner, p.29)

The ship approaches a waterfall.

Each episode of *Maakies* has a miniature 4 panel comic running along the base-line, a strip which has its own consistent characters, rules and (usually somewhat ruder) tone.[5] In one of my favourites, three poets claim to have stripped poetry of its needless pretence and fabrications to its very essentials. After two attempts, ("Hi, I!" and "A") a third claims to have written the shortest poem of all time: he shoots himself in the head. The strip

---

[5] *Krazy Kat* actually began as just one such "sideshow" strip in Herriman's 1910 comic *The Dingbat Family*.

occasionally features a mysterious tug boat inhabited by Rear-Admiral Maak, a bald, stubbly little man who resembles a fragment of Popeye. At times he is Drinky Crow's own uvula, at other times he appears in a bathroom sink which Drinky Crow (sole survivor of a violent, ten-episode rampage) is able to enter, whereupon the water darkens, the tug is surrounded by ancient and modern ships and normal service is resumed (Drinky Crow shoots himself in the head). The implication being that *Maakies* takes place in an infinitely refracted world-within-a-world, further reflected in (i) the circularity of the jokes, (ii) the shifting focus (the same gag played out on the human, animal, parasitic and macrobiotic level), (iii) fuzzy, self-justifying logic ("Sobie") and ultimately (iv) the simultaneously scabrous and poignant self-defeating loop of addiction and relapse. The unthinkable happens and the unnameable is named every single day and the next day everything has returned to normal in order for it to happen again.

Which leads us, inexorably, to 'The Farmer's Hotel'. David Berman is probably as well known as a poet as he is a songwriter – his song lyrics tend to make more use of regular rhyme schemes and Country & Western traditions, but they contain as many knock-out images as the poems, e.g. *The Natural Bridge*'s "jagged skyline of car keys" (which captures not only how much a horizontal car key resembles the silhouette of a horizon, but encapsulates the means of driving towards that horizon). 'The Farmer's Hotel' isn't like that; it's wilfully flat, starting with night falling and our narrator being lost in the one-horse town of Goshen. The song documents a gradual, apparently unalterable journey towards a place the narrator is continually warned against (or, in some cases, bemusedly directed to: "If I get your meaning then I'm definitely leaning / toward recommending the Farmer's Hotel.") The object of fear remains entirely vague. The chorus is wordless, a climbing piano and warbly guitar part. Furthermore, the melody isn't in any way ominous; the song is in a major key, heavy on flats, and captures, if anything, the narrator's tired acquiescence to his fate.[6]

> The old place it was vicious,
> Wicked and pernicious.
> "Please steer clear of that rank abattoir."
> Though her words alarmed me
> I was stuck until morning
> And in the end we must be who we are.

He arrives at the Farmer's Hotel, is given a key, even makes his way down the hallway in spite of the eerie glow emanating from the closed door. There follows an ellipsis and a reprise of the first stanza. "So now I've put an ocean / Between myself and Goshen" in order to get as far away from The Farmer's Hotel as possible. "There's no natural law / That can explain what I saw / Spread out on that straw-covered floor." We never learn, (c.f. Stella Gibbons's *Cold Comfort Farm*) what the 'something nasty' actually was, and if the effect on you is to cause you to yell, 'WHAT? WHAT WAS BEHIND THE BLOODY DOOR?' then all the better.

Eliot's 'Prufrock' has some of the best non-existent streets and passageways in all poetry: "Streets that follow like a tedious argument / Of insidious intent / To lead you to an overwhelming question... / Oh, do not ask 'What is it?' / Let us go and make our visit." (262). Eliot's second person here could be anyone who has ever complained of lack of narrative

---

[6] In fact it bears some musical resemblance to The Eagles' 'Hotel California', but with a looser, more warped melody and vocal delivery. Whereas 'Hotel California' juxtaposes supposed luxury and comfort with claustrophobia and imprisonment born of *[stifles yawn]* the trappings of celebrity ("'You can checkout any time you like, / But you can never leave.'"), the Farmer's Hotel has been selected by the narrator for its palpably foreboding, dingy qualities.

closure. What that question *is* is not the point; the tedious argument (of sinister purpose) reflects the networks of darkened streets, at once menacing and dull, leading to your inescapable destination. The question is always overwhelming, it's always sinister and we're not about to find out what it is.

Nick Cave's 'Brown Ape' (from his 13th album *Abattoir Blues/The Lyre of Orpheus*, 2004) is comparatively transparent, appearing to place us behind the 'locked door', in the middle of the cryptic text, from the first stanza. It opens:

> Farmer Emmerich went into his barn
> And found a cow suckling a serpent
> And a brown ape clanking a heavy chain
> Said Farmer Emmerich to the ape
> Never ask me to come into this barn again
> So Long
> Farewell
> So Long

The narrative plays out with clearly menacing orchestration and, as arrestingly unpleasant as it may be, the farmer has clearly walked into a symbol. Emmerich takes the animals into his home, feeds the snake 'a vat **the farmer has clearly** of milk' and tosses a dead mouse to **walked into a symbol** the ape whenever he clanks his chain. Emmerich is lynched by the villagers when they discover that he is giving succour to a serpent. The brown ape roams the forest clanking his chains in memory of the farmer. In the absence of any actual haunting, the ape becomes a kind of surrogate ghost, the world of the song suddenly and devastatingly realist. There's no such thing as ghosts and we know exactly what was in the woodshed. Happy now?

The correlation between the two absences came into relief when I was listening to the Smog song 'Keep Some Steady Friends Around' (from the totally underrated 2001 album *Rain On Lens*), a gently misanthropic number about walling up your house and garden, only letting in a few people you trust, which concludes with Bill Callahan singing:

> Someone asked me just the other day
> About souls and such
> And if I believed in Judgement Day

The song ends abruptly after the word 'day' on a single, muted note. I love that ending. It's not so much that it's none of your business (although, well, it isn't), but rather a sly intimation that it goes without saying. Indeed, it should go without saying, but whichever side Callahan (or his narrator) comes down on is anyone's guess. Of course I fucking do / don't. It's as unexpected, and as necessary, as the final scene of *The Sopranos* smash-cutting to black mid-chorus, mid-sentence: 'don't stop —'[7]

\*

John Keats, 1817: 'I mean Negative Capability, that is when man is capable of being in uncertainties, Mysteries, doubts without any irritable reaching after fact & reason.' (p. 1351)

\*

---

[7] '—believin'.'

*House MD*, episode 403: Hugh Laurie's Dr. House pages a colleague and sticks a metal knife in a plug-socket to test the theory of an afterlife. He is brought round with the message "I told you so," for his dying patient who had refused treatment on grounds of the life of the world to come.

\*

The end-credit sequence of *The Graduate*, post- grand gesture, their expressions as their breathing slows down and the shock wears off.

\*

Quite a lot of life is sitting around feeling awkward.

\*

My two favourite passages from John Ashbery's *Three Poems:*

> You know that emptiness that was the only way you could express a thing? The awkwardness around what were necessary topics of discussion, amounting to total silence on all the most important issues? That was our way of doing. (12).

and

> You know now the sorrow of continually doing something that you cannot name, of producing automatically as an apple

tree produces apples this thing there is no name for. (110).

*

The fictional space I'm talking about here is not that of endless reinterpretation. The realm opened by a poet writing a 10 by 5 table of random numbers[8] and calling it a poem is the same musty old realm opened by a schoolboy handing in a blank piece of paper for his art project:[9] the same blunt, over-

---

[8] 'The Word', published 1988, which begins "38   63   50" and continues at random. Cited by Watten in his own work of criticism, *The Constructivist Moment*, as an example of "a nonnarrative moment of expository orientation" (209-210)– by which he means the reader is forced to search for a meaning which *isn't really there* and yet, in that very abortive searching, has been conceptually manipulated by a kind of "anti-narrative", presumably in which a conceited man dupes an unsuspecting poetry reader into wasting their patience on him while he turns their expectations inside-out. The implicit defence is that the reader can interpret the poem in any way she wishes: she could decide the numbers correspond to verses from the Book of Job or the First Epistle of St. Paul to the Corinthians; she could go to London and ride the corresponding bus routes all day; she could use them as plot points on a graph. Watten is on record against Ashbery's *Three Poems* as a collection of false starts, excluding its own content, but in 'The Word' it is in this very *inclusivity* that the poem completely lacks any power or means to communicate.

[9] A season 1 episode of the unpopular NBC sitcom *My Two Dads* (Episode 13, 'The Artful Dodger', first screened 1987) concerns exactly this: one of Nicole's adoptive fathers argues that her blank canvas should have received an 'A' from her art teacher as it makes a profound statement about context, process and the state of contemporary art. That Watten's 'The Word' is published a year after this episode aired is an example of the simulacra prefiguring *the thing itself* – which is to say the thing itself was already suitably old-hat to be parodied in a prime-time, low-brow comedy screenplay without being considered over-the-heads of its prospective audience.

formulated statement about art and context, with an alarming absence of self-consciousness and a tellingly defensive line of self-analysis. Stretch it too far and it's worthless. The nature of The Black Lodge in *Twin Peaks* and the prequel movie *Fire Walk With Me* is just the right side of 'WTF?' to be endlessly engaging, have you dashing to the library to check out Jung (whom Lynch claims not to have even heard of), etc.

The current Summer exhibition at Birmingham's Ikon gallery is called *This Could Happen To You: Ikon in the 1970s*. I always find retrospectives of conceptual art a bit like waxworks of famous anti-wax industry campaigners, but that's my own baggage. TCHTY has some lastingly resonant political pieces and some lovely stuff on the prevalence of television and the industrial workplace, but what also struck me (aside from how far we haven't travelled methodologically speaking in 40 years) is the number of *Untitled*s. In one of my seminars on

**the collapse of the imagination in the face of brutality**

poetry's relation to art I ask my students to write down as many things as they can re. calling something 'Untitled'; to put themselves in the position of an artist who has just finished a piece and is going to call it *Untitled* (i.e. is not going to call it anything) or *Untitled #76*, etc. Maybe, I tell them, the work is supposed to speak for itself: a photograph of a derelict room mocked up to look like the site of political interrogation or torture. Here *Untitled* has numerous easily identifiable connotations: the collapse of the imagination in the face of brutality; an artist saying, 'Who am I to comment on this?' or 'How can I give this a title?'; a subject stripped of its familiar combination with caption and news story, unsettling effects (the artist hopes) thereof. That's fine. Call it *Untitled*. Knock yourself out.

But what if the work is (and it so very often is) some sludgy brown and grey triangles or jagged stripes which appear to have been laid on with a trowel? Maybe a couple of rips in the canvas. What does "Untitled" mean now?

*I can't be bothered to come up with a title*

is the most frequent response, cue some laughter. 'Okay,' I say, 'if the artist *wants* you to think they can't be bothered to come up with a title, what's that saying?'

*That art is pointless*

A greyish pallor sinks over the room. A couple of people usually advocate a generous 'This card has been left blank for your own message' interpretation. This is countered with an accusation of arrogance: to even claim that they're democratising culture assumes that it's theirs to democratise. They're still the one standing on the plinth, holding forth. At this point there's usually a psychology class waiting to use the room, so I say we'll continue the discussion next week, which we don't.

*

The vast majority of my friends and acquaintances are atheists and most likely, while they're too polite to say it, think I'm totally insane.

*

Our undying impulse to sing, along with Krazy Kat, "There is a heppy land furfur a-waay" with no evidence of this place which is dreamed of within a highly stylised picture of a desert.

\*

When I was a child I always ascribed a kind of talismanic power to the last pages of books. Maybe I'd been conditioned by those shitty kind of stories where in the last sentence the narrator turns out to have been a pig or a spider all along, but I would read the penultimate page (whether it was *Podkayne of Mars* or *Return of the Native*) with one hand clamped firmly over the final page, as if as if seeing one single word of it would ruin the magic, would spoil whatever conclusive answer to the riddle, punchline or convincing justification for why I had just read the book awaited me. As if that's what an ending is.

## Further reading

John Ashbery, *Three Poems* (New York: Viking Compass, 1972).

Tony Millionaire, *Maakies* (Seattle: Fantagraphics Books, 2000).

Tony Millionaire, *The House at Maakies Corner* (Seattle: Fantagraphics Books, 2002).

George Herriman, *Krazy & Ignatz 1925-1926* (Seattle: Fantagraphics Books, 2002).

Nick Cave, Nick Cave and the Bad Seeds, *The Lyre of Orpheus / Abattoir Blues* (London: Mute, 2004).

David Berman, Silver Jews, *Tanglewood Numbers* (London: Domino Records, 2005).

Bill Callahan (Smog), *Rain On Lens* (London: Domino Records, 2001).

David Foster Wallace, *Consider the Lobster* (London: Abacus, 2005).

Barrett Watten, *The Constructivist Moment: From Material Text to Cultural Poetics* (Connecticut: Weslyan University Press, 2003).

Duncan Wu, *Romanticism: An Anthology*, Edition: 3 (London: Blackwell, 2005).

Luke Kennard writes and publishes poetry and short stories. He holds a PhD in English from the University of Exeter and lectures in creative writing at the University of Birmingham. His second collection of poetry *The Harbour Beyond the Movie* was shortlisted for the Forward Prize for Best Collection in 2007. His third book is called *The Migraine Hotel* and is available from Salt. His criticism has appeared in Poetry London, The National and the Times Literary Supplement.

# POST-AVANT: A META-NARRATIVE

What is post-avant? How do you find the edge? And why is it all about sex anyway? Adam Fieled finds new pathways

Some time during the summer of 2009, I initiated a discourse on my blog, Stoning the Devil. The object of this discourse was to give the term "post-avant" concrete significations. "Post-avant" is a term with a mysterious history and an unknown etymology. Up until the discourse, no one had demonstrated the initiative to fix the term in place. That it signified, in some sense, contemporary experimental poetry, was well known; what, specifically, made post-avant poetry post-avant (rather than, say, Language poetry or Flarf) was not known.

Prior to the composition of this discourse (which was very much interactive, in a "blog," virtual context) I had devised a definition of post-avant; I called it "the diasporic movement of Language poetry towards a new synthesis with narrative and erotic elements." I still find this to be, on some levels, a viable definition, but a little top-heavy and academic to use in a blog context (where the patience of deliberate reading habits is only slowly becoming common, both for readers and writers.) The wedge I used into this discourse was something more like a sound-bite in the American press; I defined post-avant as "anything with an edge." I feel ambivalent about this move now— if "diasporic movement" was top-heavy and academic, "edge" was vague and too catch-all. But I forged ahead with "edge," and the discourse took off. Largely through links placed on a number of blogs, the discourse gained hundreds of readers, but generated mostly critical comments.

What I would like to do in this essay is explore some pieces of the discourse that still seem interesting, in a context (print anthology) that encourages patient reading and serious, formalized commentary. In the end, I believe that the post-avant discourse is more intriguing for bits and pieces it generated than for what it told its audience about this amorphous entity, "post-avant," which has still yet to generate currency or a strong foot-hold among a wide number of poets.

One primary issue that got addressed in passing, and that I find interesting, is the issue of movement-titles: specifically, whether they are ciphers or not. Here is how I chose to address the issue in the blog discourse:

> Many people continue to complain that "post-avant," as a phrase, is meaningless, a cipher. I would not necessarily disagree that "post-avant," in and of itself, is a cipher, but I do not find this to be a problem...what does "post-modern," in and of itself, mean? Whatever comes after Modernism, whatever that happens to be? What about "Romanticism" or "Symbolism"?

In the heat of the moment, I neglected to mention poetry movements to which relevant appellations have been affixed, like Objectivism and Surrealism. Many people who commented had specific complaints about the term "post-avant"; that it is logically absurd, because it is impossible to be "post" whatever "avant" is. A more thoughtful take than the one I presented on my blog (or the responses my detractors offered) might walk a middle ground between these two responses; that literary appellations used to designate movements have a so-so success ratio, when measured in terms of their resonant power. It would be nice if self-conscious literary creators could aim for the upwards target, name their movements with a certain amount of caution and deliberation; but the lesson here may be that naming movements is generally a haphazard venture. Not everything that sticks, name-wise, sticks for a reason; the arbitrary nature of the signifier is applicant even in situations when (poets think) it should not be. Other issues that came up in the context of the discourse have even more rich complications, which will move us farther from post-avant and closer, I hope, to issues with more permanent relevance.

Here is a basic issue that came up repeatedly: to be an artist (rather than merely a poet) using poetry as a means of expression, how wide does one's frame of reference need to be; to put it in another (perhaps more positive) light, what is the maximum range potential for poets (by range, I mean

## post-modernism has revolutionised the visual arts while poetry has remained virtually untouched

diversified knowledge of the arts, as arts)? I brought this up online, and I bring it up again here, because I believe that poets over the last forty years have lost something. I specifically designate fifty years because fifty years roughly corresponds to the advent of post-modernism which, despite the cipher status of its common name, has revolutionized the world of the visual arts (including film) while poetry has (arguably, at least in its mainstream manifestations) remained virtually untouched. What have been the manifestations of post-modernism in the visual arts? In large measure, straightforward painting has been marginalized, in favor of videos, installations, and conceptual pieces. In this case, it is not so much the forms but the import of the forms that matters— in these works, visual artists have made strides towards new definitions of space, bodies, sexuality, language, history, and the contentious relationship of art and politics. The only major poetry movement of the past fifty years that can make similar claims is Language poetry— however, I have seen little acknowledgement among Language poets of what these visual artists have achieved. This is important because the visual artists (from Warhol to Nauman) were mining this terrain for 15-20 years before the Language poets emerged in cohesive form in the 1980s. Moreover, visual artists like Warhol, Nauman, and more contemporary artists like Mike Kelley, Jeff Koons, and Paul McCarthy have conquered the museums, galleries, and art-markets, while Language poetry remains barely acknowledged by mainstream poetry publishers, journals, and academies. In other words, the Language poets have been considerably less successful than the visual artists in disseminating their version of post-modernism, and were beat to the punch into the bargain. All this combines to give experimental poetry the look of a lag-behind. There are good reasons to support the notion that art-forms should not compete with each other. Nevertheless, the demarcations have become so pronounced that visual artists rarely even mention contemporary poetry. I (unabashedly) believe that this is a problem. It certainly cannot be rectified by one article, but it is an issue that deserves as much attention as any nascent poetry movement.

I am proud that the discourse touched on levels more fundamental than "frames of reference" and "maximum range potentials." I made the argument that two essential constituent elements of artistic process have a preponderant quality, which much experimental poetry has denied them: subjectivity and representation. Often, an emphasis has been placed on non-representational poetry, and the stance that manifestly subjective poetry imposes a kind of closure on poems-as-constructs. There is undoubtedly some truth to these positions, especially as regards mainstream verse, which tends to lean heavily on the subjectivity of poets as a perceived wellspring of universal wisdom. Representation becomes the tool by which this wisdom is revealed to the world. Dealing with poems that I called "post-avant" or "edgy" allowed me to open up the possibility that perhaps experimental poets have thrown out too much. Poets in this milieu tend to defend their aesthetic decisions by falling back on the tenets of Deconstructionism — that words, though arbitrary, are tactile and sensuous, capable of carrying the weight of poems, series of poems, and books, in and of themselves. I find this problematic, on several levels — firstly, because I do not enjoy engaging texts that preserve what I perceive to be myths about language (that the tactility of words is sufficient to justify a thematically, narratively, and affectively impoverished text); secondly, because contemporary experimental poets have failed to win a significant number of converts, either among the general public or among wide numbers of poets; thirdly, because new generations are rising up, that are looking for fresh perspectives and novel directions; as such, I would hope that rehashing the textual ethos of an earlier movement would not seem particularly interesting. Roland Barthes discusses the necessity of *bits* of narrative, *bits* of representation; as he says, "the text needs its shadow" (32) — the novels of Robbe-Grillet demonstrate how this can be done. There are few post-modern poetry texts that raise possibilities of intermittent subjectivity and representation to the apotheosis that a text like *Jealousy* does, and all too often these texts are simply evacuated of any traces of humanity. They tend to be hermetic, and exceedingly prudish.

> dealing with poems that I called "post-avant" or "edgy" allowed me to open up the possibility that perhaps experimental poets have thrown out too much

There is a definite perversity to denying the preponderance of subjectivity and representation, and not necessarily an endearing perversity. The truth is straightforward: words not charged with at least traces of subjectivity and representational import, words which are *merely* tactile, generally hold little pleasure for most audiences.

Once it is acknowledged that subjectivity and representation are, in some senses, preponderant, questions arise as to *what* should be represented and *who* should be representing it. Much of the poetry I was writing about is both overtly narrative and explicitly sexual— thus, I argued for post-avant as a movement with "sex at the center." Central inclusion of sexuality in an art-movement seems so obvious in so many ways (sex having been at the center of most art-forms for the length of recorded history) that it may seem strange that I felt the need to argue for sex's centrality. However, I feel that the new generation of experimental poets has been, in many senses, sanitized

# I argued for post-avant as a movement with "sex at the center"

into frigidity by their teachers. So, like arguing that blinks should follow a poke in the eye, I argued for sex at the center of post-avant. The texts I used to posit this argument were ones like Brooklyn Copeland's chapbook *Borrowed House*, which uses sex as one component part of a mosaic woven of desire, dark imagery, need for intimacy and impulses to confess (which never quite shade into the melodramatic bathos of Confessionalism.) The rag and bone shop of the heart that Yeats wrote of has all the durability and permanence (not to mention tactility) of words, with the added bonus that affect, sexuality, and their representations are *not* arbitrary. They are born out of lived experience, which is (willy-nilly) as preponderant as subjectivity and representation. "Write what you know" is a pretty hoary cliché— nevertheless, like most clichés, there is a grain of truth to it. Writing what you know does not necessitate the impartation of universal wisdom, or even an attempt to do so— we can know disjuncture, ellipse, torqued forms of narrativity— but it does presuppose the preponderance of subjectivity, that I continue to argue for. Hard as it is to believe, all these home-truths (some of which border, admittedly, on platitudes) have not been spoken in an experimental poetry context in decades. In earlier contexts, they would have all the surprise of a tautology or axiom; in 2010, I hope they may be relevant, even revelatory. All these are the *what*; as to the *who*, it is my conviction that any poet (male or female) should be able to write as much about sex as they wish. The only ideology that is useful for an artist is one of complete freedom. Special interest groups want political correctness; artists (and I do not mean to romanticize the status of artists) know that there is no "correctness" in politics or anywhere else. Correctness is relative, and "correct" for an artist is whatever forms conform to the myriad shapes of subjectivities that can be manifested in text.

The problem, as I see it, is that most poets currently writing in the English language approach poetry in a way consonant with what I call minor artist strategies. They let their texts be dictated by little rule books and primers they carry around; everything must be defined, everything must be spelled out. Approaches to representation and its

**most poets let their texts be dictated by little rule books and primers they carry around**

sword-carrier, narrative, are decided beforehand; and those that do away with narrative do away with thematics into the bargain. Who wants to read poetry with no themes? Those who willfully obfuscate away from narrative build little but obsolescence into their poems. Likewise, those who take a hackneyed approach to narrative guarantee that their poems can be of no continuing interest, as invention is effaced from their discipline. That rare middle ground, where narrative approaches are concerned, in which invention is met by discipline, and old themes are endlessly refreshed, is only accessible to those who approach poetry like the major high art form it is. "Post-avant," as I have defined it, is an ideal; it occupies the space wherein that rare middle ground approach to representation can be occupied and reoccupied. These issues may be pertinent to anyone who feels that the second half of century XX saw too much taken away too fast from English language poetry; and who want to see vistas open up that can lead our poetry back to the safety of danger, the middle ground of extremes, and the timeliness of permanence.

## Further reading

Roland Barthes, *The Pleasure of the Text* (New York: Farrar Straus, 1975).
Adam Fieled, *Stoning the Devil*, http://www.adamfieled.blogspot.com (2009).

Adam Fieled is a poet based in Philadelphia. He has released four print books: *Opera Bufa* (Otoliths, 2007), *When You Bit...* (Otoliths, 2008), *Chimes* (Blazevox, 2009), and *Apparition Poems* (Blazevox, 2010) as well as numerous chaps, e-chaps, and e-books, including *Posit* (Dusie Press, 2007), *Beams* (Blazevox, 2007), and *The White Album* (ungovernable press, 2009). His work has appeared in Tears in the Fence, Great Works, The Argotist, Upstairs at Duroc, Jacket, on PennSound, in the &Now Awards Anthology from Lake Forest College Press, and an essay is forthcoming in Poetry Salzburg Review from University of Salzburg Press.

# EMILY DICKINSON, VAMPIRE SLAYER

Sophie Mayer deconstructs the metalife of a poet (whilst watching boxsets of *Buffy*)

'It is a photograph he never took, no one here took it.'
- Anne Carson, 'XLVI. Photographs: # 1748', *Autobiography of Red*

There is no extant photograph of Emily Dickinson.

About her inner life, there are very few facts: only fascicles. No facts but fragments. Jeanne Holland refers to the scriptural material of her later poems as 'scraps, stamps and cutouts.'[1] This essay proceeds by examining torn-out scraps of contemporary culture wherein Dickinson has been ascribed, aslant. I call them snapshots because they aren't. They are like the 'photograph he never took, no one here took it' that Anne Carson describes in *Autobiography of Red*, when the red-winged monster Geryon flies over an active volcano to record its growls for his ex-boyfriend's new boyfriend's documentary about Emily Dickinson.

Lyndall Gordon, in her recent biography *Lives Like Loaded Guns: Emily Dickinson and Her Family's Feuds*, suggests that Dickinson's self-imposed seclusion resulted from epilepsy, an inherited condition that we know affected her brother Austin and her nephew Ned. Her reading of the poems as an oblique symptomology makes fascinating reading, not for its truth or otherwise, but because it addresses the crux of our fascination with Dickinson: her compressed mystery. Not recluse but obtuse.

'Tell the truth but tell it slant', she wrote – and so she did. Despite a

# Emily Dickinson would not have had a Facebook page, although her cryptic lines make excellent status updates

voluminous correspondence, she confessed almost nothing. Emily Dickinson would have been useless on Big Brother. She would not have had a Facebook page, although her cryptic lines make excellent status updates. Given her love of birds, rapid communication and poetic compression, she might have Twittered. She is the subject of no biopic, with no movie tie-in edition.

Carson's title 'Photographs: # 1748' refers to Dickinson's poem numbered 1748 in the standard Johnson edition, which stands as epigraph to *Autobiography of Red*. It ends: 'The only secret people keep / Is Immortality.' Immortality has been associated with the photographic for as long as it has existed. Yet Dickinson, having had her daguerrotype taken in an era when that meant sitting still for several minutes in a standardised pose, saw photography as temporary and vulnerable to decay.

Dickinson suggests as much in a letter to Thomas Wentworth Higginson, when she noted that her father had photographs of her siblings but 'has no Mold of me, but I noticed the Quick wore off those things, in a few days.' Her formulation suggests what Roland Barthes would observe a century later in *Camera Obscura*: all photographs are (of the) dead.

Between the Mold and the Quick, Dickinson favoured the latter. She 'would not stop for Death' and yet readers have – kindly or unkindly – stopped her there. She has been cast as a haunter of graveyards, a recluse in constant mourning, a woman who looked at death the way we look at the internet: to find everything she knew. This image – the dark Angel in the House – has been fetishised, even eroticised into the original of the prim miss whose tightly-laced bodice conceals a wildly-beating heart, the smart-but-sexy librarian, the silent-but-deadly geek goth given a ravishing makeover for the prom.

## Emily Dickinson, Vampire (Slayer)

The first time I heard of Emily Dickinson was in an otherwise forgettable episode of a US sitcom (possibly *Diff'rent Strokes* spin-off, *The Facts of Life*) when a quintessentially shy-but-brilliant student at a girls' college was encouraged to write by her teacher when they discussed Dickinson's poems (think the Whitman scene in *Dead Poets' Society*, only less so). I then encountered her in *First Term at Trebizon*, a classic girls' school novel by Anne Digby, where the quintessentially shy-but-brilliant protagonist writes a poem based on Dickinson's 'There's a certain slant of light'. Dickinson's poetry has traditionally been regarded as U-rated due to the original bowdlerised edition by Mabel Loomis Todd, but it's odd that her work keeps cropping up in teen media – especially as she never made Prom Queen.

Yet she pops up again in *Buffy the Vampire Slayer*, screened in 1996 on teen TV channel The WB (home of *Dawson's Creek*), in episode four, 'Never Kill a Boy on the First Date,' the first date being between Buffy – better known for her athletic than academic ability – and the quintessentially shy-but-brilliant (and handsome) Owen, who carries a pocket edition of Dickinson at all times. Here's Owen at local hangout The Bronze trying to explain his attraction to Dickinson (and, by implication – although he doesn't know it – to the death-dealing, secret-life-having Buffy). Owen sums it up handily: she's Emo Dickinson.

OWEN:     The thing about Emily Dickinson I love is, is she's just so incredibly morbid. A lot of loss, a lot of death... It gets me. With a lot about bees, for some reason.

BUFFY:     Did she have a tragic and romantic life? With a lotta bees?

OWEN:      Quiet. Kind of sequestered and uneventful. Which I can really relate to. I... don't get out much.

Bees, of course, are an emblem not of death but of rebirth in classical poetry; Virgil thought bees were generated by corpses. After a near-death experience at the hands of a vampire, Owen declares his love for the Dickinsonian Buffy – or rather, for her frequent, violent brushes with death and the undead.

## her potential vampirism is as discernable in her poems as her epilepsy

'I never thought nearly getting killed would make me feel so... alive!' In seeing Dickinson (and bees) (and Buffy) as 'so incredibly morbid', Owen classes Dickinson as a vampire, unable to walk in daylight (Dickinson does seem to have been photosensitive, frequently writing to Susan Dickinson that she couldn't walk the short distance between their houses because it was sunny), someone tortured by impossible hungers and mired in mold. Her potential vampirism is as discernable in her poems as her epilepsy.

But what if (with a caveat that these are both allegorical states) Dickinson is not a vampire, but a vampire slayer? What if what she has to offer teen – and other – readers is her *refusal* to stop for Death and all other authorities, whether husbands, publishers or critics?' When celebrated writer Helen Hunt Jackson asked Dickinson why she had published so infrequently, Dickinson is purported to have replied to her, "How can you… [p]rint a piece of your soul!"[2] What if she set out to kill the angel in the house, not to embody it?

## Emily the Strange

The angel in the house has returned to contemporary culture, most famously in the emo guise of Bella Swan, the protagonist of Stephenie Meyer's *Twilight* series. Bella loves another tragic and reclusive Emily, Brontë, author of *Wuthering Heights*, as did Dickinson, who knew the work of that other strange Emily and was fascinated by the resonances between their lives and writing, as Susan Howe recounts so brilliantly in *My Emily Dickinson*. Like Owen, the reading public (not only the teenage female portion) appear to have been swept up in Meyer's romanticisation of nineteenth-century womanhood as passionate and tragic because repressed. Somewhere along the line, goth's and emo's (and Catherine Earnshaw's) (and Emily Dickinson's) inky, spiky rebellions against, and refusals of, the pink prettitudes of contemporary girlhood have reverted/been inverted to a melancholy (pink on the inside) swoon.

See also Fanny Brawne roaming Hampstead Heath in her mourning garb at the end of Jane Campion's *Bright Star*. Yawn. But fifteen years ago, when Campion first took on the angel in the house, she set her free through Emily Dickinson. Ada, the protagonist of *The Piano*, plays a haunting refrain on the titular instrument that is both her body and her voice, her intellect and her sexuality in one. Michael Nyman, who composed the film's music, called this rippling piano composition 'The Heart Asks Pleasure First', after one of Dickinson's best-known poems.

> The Heart asks Pleasure—first—
> And then—Excuse from Pain
> And then—those little Anodynes
> That deaden suffering—
>
> And then—to go to sleep—
> And then—if it should be
> The will of the Inquisitor
> The privilege to die—(536³).

Although the poem appears to swoon narcotically into the erotic association of sleep and death, Dickinson is not chasing a Keatsian 'drowsy numbness'. She, like Ada, places the pleasure of her heart before all else, testing and contesting 'the will of the Inquisitor,' the patriarchal figure who threatens – well, what? Ada confronts two men, one who offers love and sex and one who offers violence and death (although the film frequently misleads the viewer as to which is which). Finally, she confronts her own will, granting herself 'the privilege to die' – a death that, bee-like, is a rebirth, a final 'excuse from pain'.

## Emily de Sade

Pain is what happens when you fight the vampire; that is, when you dare to contest the vexing intersection of sex and death in Western culture. Pain is also one of the most frequent words in Dickinson's poetry. Camille Paglia calls her Amherst's Madame de Sade, reading her as experimenting on herself to discover the limits of physical and syntactic endurance. Pain is a poetics, implies Paglia; not just labour but a willed bodily extremity.

Anne Carson quotes Dickinson when parsing the meaning of the verb *lupein* (vex, harm, damage) for Sophocles' Electra, of whom she says 'Actionless she feeds on her own negativity.

## Carson is fascinated by the ever-increasing spiral of pain

"It is the only Food that Grows," as Emily Dickinson says of another equally private religion of pain.'[4] Like Paglia, Carson is fascinated by the ever-increasing spiral of pain in Dickinson's work, and by its creative function. I wonder if, for Carson, Dickinson's pain is a form of error, a signal that something is wrong that prompts the mind to pay attention, as she describes metaphor teaching us in the poem 'Essay on What I Think About Most'. Metaphor, she writes, 'causes the mind to experience itself // in the act of making a mistake.'[5] So metaphor can teach us to apprehend pain.

In her poem 'Sumptuous Destitution' (from the same collection), Carson quotes Dickinson writing to Higginson (letter 271): '*And when I try to organize – my little Force explodes – and leaves me bare and charred.*'[6] Carson's favourite metaphors are the photograph and the volcano, which both make their mark through bright, explosive forces.[7] If the volcano is the photographic flash in which the poem is made, then the '*bare and charred*' landscape – pain – is the state of the poet after making. It's also the poem: black marks on a bare surface. Here is Carson seeing the volcano in Dickinson:

> Herakles had explained that he and Ancash were travelling around South America together recording volcanoes.
> *It's for a movie*, Herakles added. *A nature film? Not exactly. A documentary on Emily Dickinson.*

*Of course*, said Geryon. He was trying to fit this Herakles onto the one he knew.
*"On My Volcano Grows the Grass,"*
Herakles went on, *is one of her poems. Yes I know*, said Geryon, *I like that poem, I like the way she refuses to rhyme* sod *with* God.[8]

Dickinson never went to Latin America; she never saw a volcano. Her poem is a photograph no one took. Her refusal to rhyme sod (grass, that which grows on the volcano; that is, the poem) with God parallels her with Emily Brontë. Carson reads the earlier Emily as contesting God, whom she calls the Whacher, for control of her own writing; resisting what Simone Weil called *decreation*, the immolation of the self in God that allows, in her interpretation, women to write. In her refusal to rhyme sod with God, Dickinson claims the grass as her own. Like bees, grass is the sign of a rebirth; it can only grow on a volcano after an eruption has enriched the soil. Grass, even if it means an eruption, is better than God. Or, as Kathy Acker frequently wrote, pain is better than dead.

## Emily, Embedded

Adam Frank argues that 'Dickinson's fascicles… and poems analogized the powers of collection and recollection that albums and photographs were coming to have in the environment of the war.'[9] Like Sally Mann's *What Remains* series of collodion photographs that includes both family portraits and the sites of Civil War battles, Dickinson's poems look at the reality of death, rather than, as the photograph has been said to do, seeking to prevent, arrest or deny it.

Dickinson lived through the Civil War yet never wrote about it.

The biggest political, economic and social upheaval for several generations passes through her life and work unmentioned, despite the fact that her father was a senator. Or so the standard accounts have us believe. Alfred Habegger notes that in 1864 several of Dickinson's poems were published (in altered versions) in *Drum Beat*, which aimed to raise funds for injured Union soldiers, and another poem appeared in the *Brooklyn Daily Union*.[10]

Jerome McGann notes something even more pertinent: 'At some point – I believe it might have been during the winter of 1861 – Dickinson decided to use her text page as a scene for dramatic interplays between a poetics of the eye and a poetics of the ear [breaking lines into two fragments]... In a very real sense modernism's subsequent experiments with its many "visible languages" are forecast in the ventures of Emily Dickinson.'[11] If McGann means the end of 1861, then Dickinson's adoption of her unconventional compositional method occurred during the 'phoney' war as Union troops blockaded the Carolinas and encamped in Virginia; if he means the end of 1860, then the change in her manuscripts occurs during Lincoln's election campaign with its promise to limit slavery.

Could Dickinson's definitive break with the conventional lineation of the era's published poetry be read as her own secession from increasing industrialisation? Or her own radical declaration of independence, her support for a campaign to end slavery – including to the mastery of the printed text? Perhaps the unusual line breaks – which begin to break words as well as phrases – demand a reader adept in wartime correspondence: a code-breaker.

Janet Holmes thinks so. The poems in her 2009 collection *The Ms. of My Kin* 'are erased from Emily Dickinson's poems of 1861 and 1862.'[12] In '1861.2' (187-192) she uncovers a coded poem that appears to speak uncannily of wars in the first decades of the twenty-first century, in that it speaks of the repetitive narrative of all wars, finding Martyrs—, Risk—,

Revelation—, Apocalypse— and Anguish.[13] What Holmes finds embedded in Dickinson's poems of 1861-62, the first, fraught years of the war when the Union army was in disarray, is not only reportage but portent, a Kassandra-like ambivalence. Women are rarely read as war poets because they do not seem to report from the front lines.

In Dickinson's urgent, capitalised and m-dashed nouns, Holmes finds a precursor not only of modernist visible language, as McGann suggests, but of a particular visible language on the frontlines of postmodernity: CNN ticker tape. In his essay on the 'running subtitle, that termite text gnawing right to left on the bottom of the screen,' Eric Cazdyn asks 'how might [the ticker tape] hint at a different form of representation, one that not only represents news and events differently but, in its most allegorical and utopian form, one that also opens up the possibility for a different shape of political representation?'[14] Dickinson offers a writing of war that is at once immediate and removed, exactly 'allegorical and utopian'.

Jerome McGann argues that the 'different shape of political representation' begins in Dickinson's compositional practice, which engages with the material world of print culture and politics. Looking at a particular uncollected manuscript page collaged with a stamp and three phrases from a review of George Sand, McGann embeds Dickinson in our contemporary dispersed, post-print culture when he notes that:

> Dickinson set up a kind of gravitational field for her writing when she fixed an uncancelled three-cent stamp (with a locomotive design) to a sheet of paper and then wrote her poem in the space she had thus imaginatively created... All of her poetry – including those few things put into print during her lifetime without her permission – was produced as handicraft work. This means that her textual medium is treated in the writing process as an end in

itself... To edit her work adequately, then, one needs to integrate the mechanisms of critical editing into a facsimile edition – which is precisely the kind of thing that codex-based editing finds exceedingly difficult to do.[15]

Like Kassandra, Dickinson was before – outside – her time, even as, in her refusal of industrialisation and politicisation, she appeared to be behind it.

## Emily, Outside(r)

Erased into prescience or heightened by hypertext: these are only two forms of contemporary response to Dickinson's work, two reflections of her decision to stand outside the marketplace. Bristol-based musicians The Wraiths included 'Wild Nights' (249) and 'She lay as if at Play' (369) on their self-produced and -distributed album

**erased into prescience or heightened by hypertext**

*Welcome,          Stranger, To    This    Place,* while American anti-folk artist Josephine Foster (half of Born Heller) recorded an entire album of Dickinson poems in simple settings that evoke the lineage from the Belle of Amherst through 1960s coffeehouse folk to contemporary psych folk. In a review of the album, Anthony D'Amico notes that *'Graphic as a Star* was conceived last winter while Foster was living in an isolated village in the mountains of Spain. She didn't bring many books with her, but one of the few that made the trip was a volume of Dickinson's poetry, which understandably resonated deeply with Josephine, given her geographic and social isolation (Emily didn't get out too much either).'[16]

D'Amico's parentheses quote Owen's observation about Dickinson in a new register, suggesting her as the model for a post-oil poet with a small carbon footprint, writing her work on domestic paper scraps and getting stitchy with them: Foster has a painting of a quilt on the cover of her album, associating Dickinson with folk arts and their current revival.

Who wouldn't want a quilted iPod cover cross-stitched with Dickinson's prescient vision:

> Musicians wrestle everywhere –
> All day – among the crowded air –
> I hear the silver strife – (#157)

I'm more tempted, though, to write with a pencil that pays tribute to artist Roni Horn's four series of aluminium columns and cubes containing black plastic letters that inscribe lines from Dickinson's work. The first series, made in 1992-93, 'How Dickinson Stayed Home', suggests both the desire and ambivalence that Dickinson's privileged home-working inspires in contemporary artists. With a room of her own and no social obligations, Dickinson was free *not* to publish, to indulge what Holland calls 'her agoraphobic withdrawal from public life.'[17] She borrows the term *agoraphobia* from Gillian Brown's *Domestic Individualism*, where it is returned to its core meaning, fear of the marketplace, in light of the fluctuating economy caused by the Civil War, which informed a converse desire to inculcate a private self impervious to market influences. Maybe Horn's aluminium bars – lightweight, minimalist, brushed-metal, almost Ikea-like in their unassuming regularity – can replace gold bars in our fluctuating economy.

## Emily, Endlessly

For those who can't afford or work aluminium, there's another (out)side to Emily. A YouTube search for 'Emily Dickinson' turns up 1520 short films, including animations of her daguerrotype reading her poems, an excerpt from a play about her domestic life called 'Every Broom & Bridget' by Tom Daley (not the Olympic hopeful), a haunting video, starring Ken and Barbie, animating Billy Collins' controversial poem 'Undressing Emily Dickinson', live recitals, paintings, and music videos for settings of her poems by composer Aaron Copeland and singer Carla Bruni.

YouTube retains something of the hypertextual nature of Dickinson's composition, and something of its homemade, handmade make-do-and-mend. Martha Nell Smith reminds us that when Dickinson sent poems to friends written on pages torn from books and magazines (she even tore up the family Bible), her generosity, both hypertextual and homemade, was (and is) endlessly generative: 'by mixing media... Dickinson also mixes tones and in doing so reminds audiences that no singleminded or singlehearted response to a subject is enough.'[18]

Perhaps the way to read Dickinson's poetry, the photograph that no-one took, is to make that photograph - poem, song, video or iPod cover - for yourself.

# Notes

[1] Jeanne Holland, 'Scraps, Stamps and Cutouts: Emily Dickinson's Domestic Technologies of Publication' (for Susan Howe), in *Cultural Artifacts and the Production of Meaning: The Page, the Image and the Body*, eds. Margaret J.M. Ezell and Katherine O'Brien O'Keeffe (Ann Arbor: University of Michigan, 1994), p. 139.

[2] Holland, p. 139.

[3] In citing Dickinson's poems, I refer to the numbering of the poems in Thomas H. Johnson's *The Complete Poems of Emily Dickinson* (New York and London: Little, Brown, 1960), although I agree with Jerome McGann that the numbering is confusing and does not reflect Dickinson's own collation of the poems in fascicles.

[4] Dickinson #1555, quoted Anne Carson, 'Translator's Foreword' in *Euripides, Electra*, trans. Anne Carson (Oxford and New York: Oxford University Press, 2001), p. 45.

[5] Anne Carson, *Men in the Off Hours* (New York: Knopf, 2000), p. 30.

[6] Ibid., p. 13.

[7] See Sophie Mayer, 'Picture Theory: On the Photographic in Anne Carson and Nicole Brossard', *Studies in Canadian Literature* 33.1 (2008), pp. 97-117.

[8] Anne Carson, 'XXXIII. Fast Forward', *Autobiography of Red* (New York: Vintage, 1998), p. 108.

[9] Adam Frank, 'Emily Dickinson and Photography', *The Emily Dickinson Journal*, 10:2, p. 15.

[10] Habegger, *My Wars Are Laid Away in Books: The Life of Emily Dickinson* (New York: Random House, 2001), pp. 402-03.

[11] Jerome McGann, 'Composition as Explanation (of Modern and Postmodern Poetries)' in *Cultural Artifacts and the Production of Meaning: The Page, the Image and the Body*, eds. Margaret J.M. Ezell and Katherine O'Brien O'Keeffe (Ann Arbor: University of Michigan, 1994), p. 120.

[12] Holmes, 'Note on the Text' in *The Ms of My Kin* (Exeter: Shearsman, 2009), np.

[13] Ibid., pp. 2-3.

[14] Cazdyn, 'A New Line in the Geometry' in *Subtitles: On the Foreignness of Film*, ed. Atom Egoyan and Ian Balfour, (Cambridge MA: MIT Press, 2004). pp. 404, 405.

[15] Jerome McGann, 'The Rationale of Hypertext,' http://www2.iath.virginia.edu/public/jjm2f/rationale.html. Accessed: 12 April 2010.

[16] Review in *Brainwashed*. http://brainwashed.com/index.php?option=com_content

&task=view&id=7977&Itemid=64. Accessed 12 April 2010.

[17] Holland, 141.

[18] Martha Nell Smith, 'The Poet as Cartoonist,' in *Comic Power in Emily Dickinson*, ed. Suzanne Juhasz, Cristanne Miller, and Martha Nell Smith (Austin: University of Texas Press, 1993), p. 81.

Sophie Mayer is the author of three books: *Her Various Scalpels* (Shearsman, 2009), *The Private Parts of Girls* (Salt, 2010) and *The Cinema of Sally Potter: A Politics of Love* (Wallflower, 2009). She enjoys writing for magazines like Chroma, Hand + Star, Horizon Review, Sight & Sound, and Staple, but frequently shares Emily Dickinson's agoraphobia.

> sophiemayer.net

# HEJINIAN'S FAUSTIENNE BEINGS-WITH[1]

Emily Critchley examines the feminist and phenomenological impulses of Lyn Hejinian's writing

> 'Along comes something – launched in context
> In context to pass it the flow of humanity divides and on the other side
>    unites
> All gazing at the stars bound in a black bow
> I am among them thinking thought through the thinking thought to no
>    conclusion'[2]

Since the 1970s Lyn Hejinian has produced a prolific array of cross-genre poetry, poetic prose and poetics that investigate mutually constitutive relationships: various interplays between poetic, critical and philosophical languages; the nature of perceptual encounters between subject and object; and interrelations between the writer and her context, including her own intellectual background. She has always been vitally concerned with both the 'motivated coincidence[s]'[3] as well as the differences within the various literary communities she has inhabited, especially those of Language poetry and the Russian avant-garde. She has participated in an impressive range of collaborations, translations and mixed-genre works since the mid-1970s, in San Francisco, Berkeley, and New York City, and in Leningrad-St. Petersburg since the 1980s.[4] In Hejinian's own words: 'To trace the lines of reciprocity through which [meaningfulness and meaning...] are established is to map a social space, a community.'[5] Her writing often bears witness to specific occasions that prompted literary activity within these communities, such as readings, talks, calls for papers, translations, and so on, as well as the people with whom she has collaborated or for whom she has written.

Her by now quite well-known book of poetics, *The Language of Inquiry*, is a compilation of such papers, talks, correspondences and poems. In its introduction Hejinian writes:

> Like George Oppen, I am aware that poets work in the context of 'being numerous.' These essays were prompted by invitations and called into existence by occasions, but their true context is a community – literary and pedagogical – in which challenges and encouragement, provocations and excitement, contention and insights have been generated over the years in a mode which I would define as friendship of the most supreme kind.[6]

Hejinian has long been recognized for her active support of other poets within the experimental community or, better, communities – many of whom she published through her own press, Tuumba, which she ran for eight years (1976-84). She was also joint editor, alongside Barrett Watten, of *Poetics Journal* from 1981 to 1999. More recently she became co-director of Atelos, a literary project commissioning and publishing a wide variety of cross-genre work. Her encouragement of other female poets in particular, in the form of publications, but also through private letters and emails, has only recently started to be discussed in detail, for instance, by Ann Vickery in *Leaving Lines of Gender*,[7] and by Nicky Marsh who writes of the 'lengthy but largely private' 'battle' that was Hejinian's 'vigorous' attempt 'to make Language writing's literal poetic community aware of the gendering of its own practices.'[8]

Her quite central place within the Language grouping, arguably unparalleled amongst female writers, was achieved early on in the group's formation due to her active self-identification with and promotion of the practices of that community. For instance, her work shows a major investment in many of the formal, political and philosophical concerns of other Language writers, such as a focus on leftist politics, philosophy and the defamiliarizing literary strategies of poetic predecessors – the Objectivist poets and Gertrude Stein to name perhaps the two most important. Yet, as much as she has always been identified with the Language group, Hejinian's writing resists some of the more extreme or abstract theories of her male Language peers.[9] Instead of denying representation or authorial subjectivity, for example, her poetic explorations of notions of the writer's self and the 'lived' experience, in phenomenological terms, has always given her work

## Hejinian investigates an 'embedded' female subjectivity

a subjective element that other Language writing at times lacks.[10] Her investigations into subjectivity and, in particular, an 'embedded,'[11] female subjectivity, which is personal at the same time as intellectual, actively engaged and political, are especially encouraging to the feminist reader of Language poetry. For instance, her multiple and sometimes conflicting positions as a Language writer, a feminist, a thinker, a wife and a mother simultaneously have meant that Hejinian has lived out, quite literally, most of the different possibilities of ontologically 'being-with' under discussion here. As she explains in her paper 'Language and "Paradise"': 'The parenthetical plural is always part of her condition. And her subject-object, I-we, public-private status becomes ever more pronounced in the "unconventional position" which constitutes the writing posture.'[12]

Much of Hejinian's thinking and writing has focused on dialectical overlaps between the political and personal, or the literary and the lived, both sides of which can be realms of intellectual concern if approached with thorough-going self-awareness. Due, perhaps, to the need for such complex negotiations between different subject positions, her writing has remained resistant to the kind of authoritarian, single-minded or abstract tendencies which Language poetics ostensibly eschewed, but which, as I have explored

## a poetry of careful epistemology

elsewhere, much of it ended up reproducing.[13] As Hejinian puts it in *My Life in the Nineties*: 'One wants one's work to be shareable – one seeks the shareable (*not* universal).'[14] Instead, she has argued for a poetry of careful epistemology,[15] but one which is radically 'contextual and always shifting'[16] – one that constitutes a specifically *female* mode of thinking, which Hejinian termed 'La Faustienne.'[17]

Though Hejinian invokes thinking from a wide variety of intellectual 'movements' – especially Language writing and phenomenology, but also Russian formalism, Objectivism, the Frankfurt school, feminism, and so on – she deliberately writes away from any single perspective or totalising intellectual system, always attempting, instead, to question and transgress the boundaries with which any political or philosophical stance is cordoned off. Consequently, her work is hard to 'fix' critically. It requires wilful immersion in its suspension of many of the markers of causality, 'aboutness' and value. For Hejinian constantly shifts the boundaries of both content and intent, of inside and outside, in her writing; as she puts it: '"aboutness" (in poetry, but [...] also in life) is transitional, transitory.'[18] She has written repeatedly of an ambivalence of intention in both her poetry and her poetics: these being the important spaces, for her, in which encounters with the world, with variant and unforeseen events, including meaning, especially the meaning and meaningfulness of others, can take place. For instance, she writes about how 'the swirl of meaningfulness' which is 'part of the ongoing course of one's daily living among others'[19] only becomes visible within a mode of reduced intentionality, which lets otherness appear.

Writing on Stein's *Stanzas in Meditation* Hejinian notes that 'there is a difference between thinking *about* and thinking, and thinking itself is meaningful too' (italics mine).[20] Later in the same essay she articulates the specifically phenomenological thrust of this understanding:

> the substance of the [*Stanzas in Meditation*...] is the recurrent coming into appearance, the phenomenology, of meanings, the varieties of meanings, the demands of meanings, the endless and difficult meaningfulness that faces one everyday. The meditation is not simply a response to meaning; rather, it is the articulation of being in meaning – in the stream of meaning.[21]

The water imagery used here: 'stream,' 'swirl,' 'ongoing course,' may have its roots in what William James repeatedly referred to as 'the stream of consciousness' in his writings. Hejinian muses on his analyses of consciousness in 'Two Stein Talks,' though she records her own experience of consciousness as, conversely, 'broken up, discontinuous – sometimes radically, abruptly, and disconcertingly so.'[22] On the other hand, this disjunction between the self and the self experiencing consciousness of the self exists, for Hejinian, within a larger continuum, that of lived experience per se.

Hejinian's work thus embraces a Steinian brand of realism (itself influenced by Stein's studies in psychology under William James), one that is inclusive, not conclusive, as well as vulnerable, shifting and uncertain – based on the ever-changing dynamics of perception itself. Yet such uncertainty, rather than precluding a sense of hope or affirmation is, on the contrary, the very sign of full living for the writer. As she explains in 'Reason,' to be lodged in 'doubt,' 'dilemma' and self-questioning, is to be on the way to 'affirmation of our deepest reason, the one that tells us that things and our experiences of them count.'[23] Moreover, Hejinian frequently rescues the positive connotations of the word 'ambivalence', denoting, not a situation of either / or, but both simultaneously, for instance in the following, from her poem *Slowly*:

> I can't help but yield philosophically to the proliferation of detail, the endless distinctions, large and small, deliberately producing contradictions, irreconcilability, and, in me, irresolution, so that I can only offer ambivalence happily in place of conviction – evasiveness, prevarication, the presentation of things that are abruptly otherwise...[24]

Thus is it necessary for Hejinian to maintain a 'healthy dialectic between poetry and poetics,' as she writes in *My Life*,[25] one that crucially upsets the object relations of traditional, academic analysis, from the perspective of which 'poetry stands at a distance, objectified and under scrutiny.'[26] However, against a Derridean move toward '(a rhetorical)' aporia or, in Hejinian's terms, 'the famous (or notorious) postmodern (or postpostmodern) negativity [...] a gap of meaning,'[27] Hejinian's emphasis on perceiving relations between and with phenomena is always as an activity through which humans can come to know one another and themselves – a concept she inherited from phenomenologists James, Heidegger, Arendt and Merleau-Ponty, as well as from Stein and Oppen. As the latter wrote:

> There are things
> We live among 'and to see them

Is to know ourselves'...[28]

Or as Hejinian puts it in her introduction to *Inquiry*: 'It is at points of linkage – in contexts of encounter […] that one discovers the reality of *being in time*, of *taking one's chance*, of *becoming another*, all with the implicit understanding that *this is happening.*'[29] Via such an intellectual context Hejinian has arguably built upon phenomenological (and specifically, Stein's) explorations of subjectivity and gender, and developed a contemporary, feminist, poetics of the 'third-wave,': a poetics that is active, philosophical and self-aware, whilst being always contingent, at times contradictory, and definitively non-definitive.

In place of rationalistic principles of certainty, objectivity and generalizability, Hejinian's writing discovers knowing to be an ongoing activity, a perpetual coming-to-know, or 'not-yet-knowing,'[30] characterized by self-questioning, doubt and strangeness, during which the perceiver comes to recognize both the object under perception and herself as 'other.' With reference to what Oppen described as 'O's affirmation': the 'curiosity – "care, concern" – which makes […] things count,'[31] Hejinian describes the activity of mind she calls 'doubt' as 'not entirely unlike what Keats called negative capability';[32] in other words, an intentional open-mindedness that puts us in co-existence with uncertainties and that which cannot be resolved or understood through reason.[33] This sense of being-with or, as Hejinian always puts it, 'coinciding' with things, forms the basis of her writing, i.e., the dynamic of our happening to notice things, our coming into co-existence momentarily with them, but stopping short of the need to know, categorize or contain them.

Such a process of acknowledgment, rather than pretending to a comprehensive knowledge, has important ethical connotations, because it allows for the affirmation and value of things and persons, such as 'women and other "others,"'[34] without submitting them to conceptual objectification (the first stage in hierarchization?). In 'Barbarism,' for instance, Hejinian cites an essay by Peter Nicholls on Oppen, entitled 'Of Being Ethical,' noting its influence on her own poetics.[35] 'Such a "poetics of encounter,"' Hejinian writes, employing Nicholls' phrase, 'has an ethical dimension, since it is established within relationships expressing proximity rather than contemplative or legislative distance.'[36] Feminist philosophers such as Carol Gilligan and Martha Nussbaum have understood that the subsection of philosophy entitled ethics has long been grounded in a patriarchal, masculinist definition of 'reason', of the type that Hejinian continually challenges – for instance, in her essay of the same name.[37] *Her* poetics, conversely, tends toward something more like virtue theory,[38] which insists that morality is not about conforming to a set of infallible, objective rules, but about being trained to see problematic situations in a moral way.

The poet's creative explorations along such a border of ethics and aesthetics in part accounts for the emphasis on haecceity or 'thisness' throughout her oeuvre, which she shares with Oppen and Stein, in place of symbolic categorisations, because, as she puts it: 'To know *that* things are is not to know *what* they are, and to know *that* without *what* is to know otherness (i.e., the unknown and perhaps unknowable).'[39] (To state that a rose is a rose is a rose tells us nothing much – and yet how much! – about that particular flower.) It also accounts for the 'spirit of provisionality'[40] in which Hejinian has always written, and the importance to her work of contradiction and paradox. Such a stake in dynamic and contradictory opposites shows the poet's commitment to an alternative dialectics, or processes of 'assimilation,' in Hejinian's words, 'where opposites as such can't exist because they always coexist.'[41]

In 'The Quest for Knowledge in the Western poem'[42] and 'La Faustienne' Hejinian explicates the familiar feminist argument that the need to know is, on some level, a need to contain or possess, and identifies the trail of destruction this dynamic has left historically. Both of these essays differently ask the question 'What does a poem know?' and, in the process, identify the search for a 'body of knowledge' as being 'a peculiarly Western construct.'[43] Hejinian offers this body in terms of the conquest of a geographical landmass, specifically Columbus' 'discovery' of America, the mythologized Faust's desire for a comprehensive knowledge of everything, and the gendered or erotic dominance that men have sought over women. She identifies the quest for 'obtaining and securing' knowledge as the driving force of occidental study for the last thousand or so years.[44]

Her response to such a 'force' in 'The Quest for Knowledge' is to uncover and explore areas of 'unsettlement and disorientation.'[45] Formally, the essay is comprised of poetry intermixed with sections of expository prose based on notes that were written to parallel the poetry. Such a form is disorienting in itself and in some ways affirms and enacts Hejinian's subject of estrangement from certainty. The focus is on **the contingent, culturally-constructed nature of knowledge**: 'Western knowledge itself has been a set of inventions, framed by perception but linked to anticipation' Hejinian writes;[46] hence the poet's passion for alternative viewpoints. In Hejinian's case, this has been most explicit in her multiple voyées into Russian thinking, writing and translating, which resulted in, amongst other works, *Oxota: A Short Russian Novel*.[47] In stark contrast to the omniscience of the narrator in many Western novels, *Oxota*'s narrator is marked by a sense of dislocation and disorientation, which Hejinian describes in 'The Quest for Knowledge' as 'very much a Russian theme.'[48] Hence too her desire to undercut the 'simulacrum of stability of both locale and self' that, in her view, has reached a damaging peak in the ideational construct of the Western world. As she writes in 'The Person and Description':

> The individual is a figure that steadfastly, in Western culture, appears at the apex of hierarchical structures; it stakes its claims on them and establishes itself as their dominating figure. [...T]he notion of 'identity' – the identity of the individual – is itself party to a hierarchical structure, one in which 'identity' governs the question of who an individual might be. And yet, even as identity is a governing factor, it is a limiting factor too. [49]

Throughout her work, especially in *A Border Comedy*,[50] *The Cold of Poetry* [51] and *The Cell*,[52] Hejinian reconfigures such concepts of person and place, such as the 'I' and 'the West' (still referring to the Western world), which are often perceived to be dominant, self-contained entities, showing them to be constantly shifting border-zones, fundamentally contextual and perspectival:

> Above our real things the corresponding sky drifts toward the edge of the
>     dark [...] as the sunset, claiming the horizon, binds it (by whatever
>   is to come, whatever to continue) to the West.
>       It is faced by an unbacked bench.
>       The West?
>       It is met with perception.
>       Set with appreciation.
>       And I am one
>       Until I'm placed in the objective sense – am I to say 'prepared'? – a
>               person to turn sky around sun.
>       An enclosure?

Knowledge?

[…] Still, I would get rid of *I* if I could, I said, I did, I went.[53]

The image of the horizon offered in this extract is both pictorial – the edge of sky at which the sun sets – and metaphorical. In the mode of Heidegger, who was preoccupied with rediscovering pre-Socratic thinking and with hermeneutical horizons of meaning, especially in *Being and Time*,[54] and also of Gadamer, who claimed that all understanding takes place within a certain 'horizon' that is historically conditioned, partial, perspectival, and situated in language, Hejinian discerns knowledge to be a series of borders or horizons that we claim for ourselves, perceptions of which can become frozen in time. Such borders include, for example, the era of Socrates and Aristotle, which gave rise to logic and ratiocentric thought, and the Age of 'the so-called Enlightenment'[55] as Hejinian describes it. For example:

[T]he moment when the West distinguished itself from the rest, is often said to have occurred between 500 and 399 B.C., in the century of Socrates, the period that defined and established the concept that fundamental laws might be discovered and incontrovertible logic be constructed for governing philosophy, science, and the social state.

[…]

But in considering contemporary experience, and particularly contemporary notions of what and how we know […] an attempt to observe the West should be equally attentive to the fundamental redefinition and reevaluation of the rules of knowing…[56]

In 'La Faustienne' in particular, Hejinian investigates the gendered implications of traditional notions of knowledge and selfhood as complete and self-identical entities. Whilst acknowledging 'a certain heroic quality to the Faust figure'[57] – the quintessence of one whose insatiable desire for the acquisition and accumulation of knowledge proves his undoing –

**the heroism of Faust is compromised**

Hejinian decides that such heroism is 'so compromised that is seems to be an ultimately irrelevant heroism – misbegotten and probably contemptible.'[58] Instead, she champions a model of knowledge represented by Scheherazade, a figure who *makes* knowledge, rather than simply acquiring it, with her 'creative and redemptive power'[59] – which power is closely bound up with the productive, literary imagination. After reading Sir Richard Burton's 1886 translation of *The Arabian Nights*,[60] Hejinian tells us, she realized she had found La Faustienne. Her explicit gendering of these different models of knowledge is quite fascinating in the context of her own position as a female writer of Language poetry. This essay appears to be her attempt to grapple explicitly with feminist issues - which she elsewhere problematizes - in the semi-mythologized, semi-historical space afforded her by the figures Faust and Scheharazade, as well as the neutralized realm, as she sees it, of night.

'La Faustienne' charts the story of the real-life Faust, whose tragedy has become world-famous, but whose real value, for Hejinian, lies in its representativeness of 'the history of plunder and exploitation that Western knowledge-seekers have left behind them.'[61] The 'bachelor,' 'scholar,' 'scientist and doctor,' 'consumed by love of knowledge which is transmuted into an overwhelming desire to know "everything"' is 'a familiar figure,' according to Hejinian.[62] He is responsible both for ransacking Donne's 'new-found world,' (the American continent) and simultaneously figuring such territory in terms of a female othering: as virgin, Paradise, mother, Eve, and so on. Hejinian: 'Throughout the literature of the frontier, the intrepid

Faustian discovers a *virgin landscape* and penetrates its wilderness [...] the unknown is imagined as an animate (though supine) other and she is female. The female element in this trope, then, is not the knower but the site of knowledge, its object and embodiment – that which is to be known.'[63]

This linguistic tendency goes both ways of course. Otherness, Hejinian explains, has tended to be personified as female. Woman has been the traditional object of the well-documented male gaze throughout history.[64] Thus knowledge and the unknown have been sexualized and, the implication is, the need to contain woman, upheld. As Hejinian puts it: 'The erotic site is, then, a secret site – and it is, too, a threatening one, since it is also a source of power [...] Sexuality becomes the site of questions about what can and cannot be known.'[65] Hejinian's questioning in these two essays of 'the dualism that is the basis for much of our Western thinking'[66] is productive. It leads to her search for and discovery of a place where such binary thinking can be complicated – her 'night work':

> [M]y interest is in the processes of assimilation and assessment that take place in the figurative dark and silence of night, where opposites as such can't exist because they always coexist. I have wanted to write in the dark, so to speak, when the mind must accept the world it witnesses by day and out of all data assemble meaning. The writing would do so – assemble (a Faustian project) and in its way *make* knowledge (the work of La Faustienne).[67]

Here at night when her mind is less intentional and more open, 'to dreams and the imagination', Hejinian allows her semi-consciousness to '*make* knowledge' rather than simply to assemble what it already knows.[68] In other words, Hejinian is intent on enacting the Faustienne dynamic for herself:

The bed is made of sentences which present themselves as what they are

Some soft, some hardly logical, some broken off

Sentences granting freedom to memories and sights

Then is freedom about love?

Bare, and clumsily impossible?

Our tendernesses give us sentences about our mistakes

Our sentiments go on as described

[…]

The bed shows with utter clarity how sentences in saying something make
                    something

Sentences in bed are not describers, they are instigators…[69]

Such a poem, situated unexpectedly in the middle of her essay, traces Hejinian's interest in recounting and exploring things as 'they are': illogical ('hardly logical') erroneous ('our mistakes') and fragmentary ('broken off'), which the poet associates with 'freedom,' and with 'love' – followed by a question mark, i.e., uncertainly. The last couple of sentences in the extract also reflect her poetic method more generally: letting the language itself spark new ideas, lead to new beginnings, rather than employing words to fit exactly pre-defined meanings. The most important lesson the 'wise and subtle' Scheherazade teaches the King Shahryar, Hejinian goes on to say, is 'that every man is at the call of Fate' rather than fully in control of it.[70] This is a highly significant moral for Hejinian and resonates in the context of her work as a whole, with its emphasis on epistemological uncertainty and vulnerability in the face of otherness. As she puts it at the end of 'La Faustienne,' in 'A Fable' dedicated to another female Language poet and feminist, Carla Harryman, 'Various women writers will take up the philosophical quest for uncertainty.'[71]

# Notes

[1] 'Being with' (*Mitsein*) is a Heideggerian formulation from the fourth chapter of his *Being in Time*, trans. John Macquarrie & Edward Robinson (Oxford: Blackwell, 1962). 'La Faustienne' is Hejinian's feminist take on the traditional Faustian quest for knowledge – as explicated later in this essay.

[2] Lyn Hejinian, *Happily* (California: Post-Apollo Press, 2000), 5.

[3] Hejinian, *The Language of Inquiry* (Berkeley: University of California Press, 2000), 328. (Hereafter: *Inquiry*)

[4] For instance, with other Language poets Leslie Scalapino, Barrett Watten, Carla Harryman, Kit Robinson, Michael Davidson and Ron Silliman, musician John Zorn, painter Emile Clark and director Jacki Ochs. Hejinian has also translated the work of Russian writers Arkadii Dragomoshchenko and Ilya Kutik.

[5] Hejinian, *Inquiry*, 38.

[6] Ibid., 4.

[7] Ann Vickery, *Leaving Lines of Gender: A Feminist Genealogy of Language Writing* (Hanover, New Hampshire: Wesleyan Press, 2000).

[8] Nicky Marsh, 'Infidelity to an impossible task: postmodernism, feminism and Lyn Hejinian's My Life,' *Feminist Review*, 74, 'Fiction and Theory: Crossing Boundaries' (2003), 70-80, 70.

[9] Cf. Ron Silliman's 'The New Sentence', Bruce Andrews' Text and Context', Charles Bernstein's 'Artifice of Absorption' and Steve McCafferey's 'The Death of the Subject' for examples of some pretty grandiose, if rhetorical, claims.

[10] Her most well-known work, the prose poem *My Life* (Los Angeles: Sun & Moon Press, 1987), certainly has autobiographical elements (though is still far from being 'autobiography' as most people would understand the term), not least in its structure: one section for each year of Hejinian's life. Lisa Samuels has usefully described it as 'autography', and points to its having been 'doubly *motivated* – by the personal and the literary – in a kind of arithmetics of autobiography'. Samuels, 'Eight justifications for canonizing Lyn Hejinian's *My Life*': http://epc.buffalo.edu/authors/samuels/mylife.html#1.

[11] I mean 'embedded' here in the sense theoretically treated by the third-wave feminist, Judith Butler, for whom the 'subject' is culturally constructed, but nevertheless

vested with an agency, usually figured as the capacity for reflexive mediation, that remains intact regardless of its cultural embeddedness. *Gender Trouble: Feminism and the Subversion of Identity* (New York & London: Routledge, 2006; first published in 1990).

[12] Hejinian, *Inquiry*, 70-71.

[13] Emily Critchley, 'Dilemmatic boundaries: constructing a poetics of thinking,' *Intercapillary / Space* (online, November 2006) and '[D]oubts, Complications and Distractions': Rethinking the Role of Women in Language Poetry', *Hot Gun! Journal*, #1, ed. Josh Stanley (Summer 09), 29-49.

[14] Hejinian, *My Life in the Nineties* (NY: Shark Books, 2003), 67.

[15] Hejinian: 'Poetry [...] is fundamentally an epistemological project [...But] the nature of knowing [...] is circumstantially embedded.' *Inquiry*, 296.

[16] Ibid.

[17] See Hejinian's essay of that name, ibid., 232-67.

[18] Ibid., 2.

[19] Ibid., 365.

[20] Ibid., 356.

[21] Ibid., 365.

[22] Ibid., 103.

[23] Ibid., 351.

[24] Hejinian, *Slowly* (California: Tuumba Press, 2002), 37.

[25] Hejinian, *My Life* (Los Angeles: Sun & Moon Press, 1987, 64.

[26] Hejinian, *Inquiry*, 1.

[27] Ibid., 340.

[28] Cited by Hejinian, ibid., 347.

[29] Ibid., 3.

[30] Ibid., 269.

[31] The parallels with Heidegger's concept of 'care' (*sorge*) or 'care for others' (*fursorge*) as a condition of 'being with' are also worth mentioning here.

[32] Hejinian, *Inquiry*, 351.

[33] 'When man is capable of being in uncertainties, mysteries, doubts without any irritable reaching after fact and reason.' Keats's letter to George and Thomas Keats dated Sunday, 21 December 1817. Nathan Scott notes that negative capability has been compared to Heidegger's concept of 'Gelassenheit,': 'the spirit of disponibilité before What-Is which permits us simply to let things be in whatever may be their uncertainty

and their mystery' in *Negative Capability: Studies in the New Literature and the Religious Situation* (New Haven and London: Yale University Press, 1971).

[34] Hejinian, *Inquiry*, 38.

[35] Ibid., 332. Nicholls reads Oppen through the phenomenology of Levinas, whose notion of 'sincerity' had significant impact on the Objectivist poets.

[36] Ibid.

[37] Ibid., 337-54.

[38] Exponents of aspects of 'virtue theory' include Gilligan and Nussbaum, the latter of whose *Love's Knowledge* (Oxford University Press, 1992) sees literature as a way of testing moral theory to see if it 'works.'

[39] Hejinian, *Inquiry*, 2.

[40] Ibid., 4.

[41] Ibid., 250.

[42] Ibid., 209-31.

[43] Ibid., 211-12.

[44] Ibid., 215.

[45] Ibid., 209.

[46] Ibid., 212. Cf. Heidegger's *Being and Time*, § 1.

[47] Hejinian, Lyn, *Oxota: A Short Russian Novel* (Massachusets: The Figures, 1991).

[48] Hejinian, *Inquiry*, 209-10.

[49] Ibid., 199.

[50] Hejinian, Lyn, *A Border Comedy* (New York: Granary Books 2001).

[51] Hejinian, Lyn, *The Cold of Poetry* (Los Angeles: Sun and Moon Press, 2000).

[52] Hejinian, Lyn, *The Cell* (Los Angeles: Sun and Moon Press, 1992).

[53] Ibid., 212.

[54] For instance, Heidegger's 'horizon' as 'the side facing us of an openness which surrounds us.' 'Conversation on a Country Path about Thinking, *Martin Heidegger: Discourse on Thinking*, trans. John M. Anderson and E. Hans Freund (NY: Harper and Row), 64.

[55] Hejinian, *Inquiry*, 233.

[56] Ibid., 214.

[57] Ibid., 233.

[58] Ibid.

[59] Ibid.

[60] Richard Burton, *Arabian Nights: Tales from a Thousand and One Nights* (New York: Modern Library, 2001).

[61] Ibid., 236-37.

[62] Ibid., 237.

[63] Ibid., 240.

[64] Cf. *The Female Body in Western Culture*, ed. Susan Rubin Suleiman (Cambridge, MA: Harvard University Press, 1985), and Lynda Nead's *The Female Nude: Art, Obscenity and Sexuality* (London and New York: Routledge, 1992) for more detailed examinations of this.

[65] Hejinian, *Inquiry*, 247. Think of the misogyny equating the excesses of a woman's body with her supposed inferiority of mind that runs throughout the writings of Ovid, Juvenal, Biblical scripture, Aristotle, the early Church Fathers, Tertullian, Ambrose, Jerome, Augustine, Aquinas – much of which served as the foundation of Western thought.

[66] I.e., man with mind, woman with matter, *à la* Aristotle. Ibid., 249. Cf. Hélène Cixous' 'Sorties: Out and Out: Attacks/WaysOut/Forays' for a neat deconstruction of this and other binaries. *The Newly Born Woman*, transl. Betsy Wing (University of Minnesota Press: Minneapolis, 1986), 63-132.

[67] Hejinian, *Inquiry*, 250.

[68] Ibid.

[69] Ibid., 250-51.

[70] Ibid., 255.

[71] Ibid., 261.

Emily Critchley gained a PhD in contemporary American women's experimental writing and philosophy from the University of Cambridge, where she was the recipient of the John Kinsella & Tracy Ryan Poetry Prize in 2004. She teaches English & Creative Writing at the University of Greenwich. She has several chapbooks published with Torque Press, Oystercatcher, Dusie, Bad Press and Arehouse, and is one of the featured poets in *Infinite Difference: Other Poetries by UK Women Poets* (Shearsman, 2010). She has a book forthcoming with Penned in the Margins in 2011.

# THESE TERABYTES I HAVE TRIED TO SHORE AGAINST OUR RUINS

Digital poetics, the modernist project and modes of cognition: Theodoros Chiotis joins the dots

1

It is unfortunate that computers increase the work for us to do; in the digital world the act of opening the book is replaced by the act of unboxing, plugging in, shuffling around the contents of a data interface (usb stick, browser, etc). Natural and artificial languages join in ways previously unheard of. Without moving, the reader-user traces a line joining together fragments and segments of text, image, video, animation; in this manner, alternate geographies of language, identity and textuality are created. The image of the book as an artifact with well-defined boundaries is replaced by a never-ending flow of flickering images. The world projected on a screen is splintered and cracked; the established confines of poetic discourse now yield to all other types and genres of textual (and artistic) discourse. Similar ruptures have already taken place in other artforms. When the processes of recording sound were introduced into music in the twentieth century as musical elements themselves, it resulted in the redefinition of what music was and what it could do. In much the same way, the implementation of audiovisual components and, more importantly, programming language into literary discourse redefines dramatically what text might be able to do.

The act of reading and writing poetry has become a more intricate process as it has to thread together a number of different technologies, practices and languages in its attempt to become a multidimensional, interdisciplinary performance. Considerations of the metatextual, metalinguistic, architectural and conceptual dimensions of the poetic work are paramount in the digital environment. The uprooting of the poem from its previously fixed incarnation endows it not only with movement but also with variable speeds; oscillating as it does between text, sound, animation and video recording. The cognitive surplus produced by the information overload inevitably results in the invention of new ways of navigating the projection of text on the browser: new ways of reading. It is the mediation of literary discourse and the remoulding of our cognitive capabilities and affective capacity that delimits my short discussion.

### reading and writing poetry has become a multidimensional, interdisciplinary performance

2

You use the typewriter or the word processor to type out your poetry without letting the tool interfere with the art form itself in any sort of direct manner. The word processor is an instrument of writing but never a component of the compositional process. The Muse might interfere with the writing process turning the poet into her own instrument of writing but the Muse is a higher power ensuring the resulting narrative will last through the ages. The writing tools used by the poet belong to a lower ontological stratum (i.e. they are seemingly non-sentient) and should therefore not be allowed to interfere with the art work. This romantic, even luddite, concept reinforces the human agent in the act of writing poetry by establishing the Author as the originator not just of poetry but of the entire continuum of language. More than anything else, the author attests to the existence of a irrefutable message ensconced within a literary work.

The emergence of digital literature firmly refuted the concept of the author as the originator of any incontrovertible truths folded within a literary work and, by extension, all discourse. The existence of an author, Michel Foucault slyly noted, is the principle of thrift in the proliferation of meaning. The removal of the human agent as the sole originator of discourse changes things dramatically. Programming code concealed as it is beneath multiple strata of technological devices initiates decisions and produces effects the programmer did not consciously consider. Long before the advent of digital literature there were works such as Optatianus Porphyrius' *Carmina* which appeared as early as the first quarter of 4th century AD or Julius Caesar Scaliger's *Poetices* (1561) employing combinatorial compositional methods to either conceal within them narratives to be discovered by those with the key or to create endless permutations of the same poems; in both cases, man was displaced from the centre of production of meaning and its regulation.[1] These works are only a small selection of similar texts acting

## the principle of thrift in the proliferation of meaning

as precursors to print works such as Roussel's 1274-line poem *Nouvelles Impressions d' Afrique* (first published in 1932), Roubaud's *Le Grand Incendie de Londres* (first published in 1989)[2] or digital poems such as Stephanie Strickland and Cynthia Lawson Jaramillo's *Vniverse*[3] and Jim Andrews' *Enigma n.*[4] In all of these four pieces what used to be merely a method or a series of constraints has become a process-based approach to the writing of poetry and by extension the production of meaning. Whereas a book is the vessel of a printed poem, the computational environments in which digital poems are embedded enable structural mappings across domains; as the computational environments traverse from analogue to digital, they become separate parts of a dynamic system of textuality. It follows that the configuration and distribution of the work in a computational environment become additional structural features of the poetic work. Together they form a meta-machinic assemblage.[5] For example, Nick Monfort's *ppg256*,[6] a series of poetry generators using the Perl programming language, depend on the existence of a standard Perl interpreter and a human agent who will type in the Perl commands and read the resulting poems. Montfort notes that this project "deals with the poet's cognition in composition, the programmer's cognition in programming, the reader's cognition in understanding how a program works, and the reader's cognition in reading poems".[7] The presentation of the poems generated by the programming language also doubles as a presentation of the forces generating meaning operating on and interacting with each other. Human and machine languages become enmeshed. The operative dimension of the poetic work becomes an inseparable component of its aesthetic nature, embedded in both physical (machine) and immaterial (language) space.

3

The poetic works operating within these flows of compounded meaning-processes make tangible the minute processes of human imagination as well; more importantly, however they also offer the reader-user the possibility of mapping spaces in the interstices of textuality. If, as Anne Sexton has often inferred, poetry acts as an index of the

## the "I" in digital poetry is a sea of larval selves

unconscious of the poet, then the "I" in digital poetry is a sea of larval selves, a population of processes, where the self-as-poet-and-reader dips in and out of a multitude of screens, engaging with languages and multiple strata of processes he does not fully grasp.

4

Anyone who has ever used video or music recorders, mobile phones, computers or word processors is aware that human and machine interaction result in the extension of both parties in each other's worlds. Digital poetry forces us amongst other things to rethink the concept of machines as being external to humans. In digital poetry the image of the ghost in the machine might be more accurately replaced by the image of a ghostly-reader moving within the poem at the same time that the poem is moving inside the ghostly-reader; poem and reader are engaged in an attempt to read each other. In an essay of 1966, John Cage suggested that "what we need is a computer that isn't labor-saving but which increases the work for us to do, that puns.... as well as Joyce revealing bridges.....where we thought there weren't any, turns us.....not 'on' but into artists".[8] Sense is created in the spaces between transitions every time the digital poem is accessed and experienced. Sense is dependent on computer processing time and human perception, a kind of temporal knowledge we use to feel with and that poet-programmers are exploring in new and unexpected ways.[9] Man and machine, natural and artificial languages haunt one another.

5

The invention of the first reading machine dates to the sixteenth century and is credited to Agostino Ramelli. Ramelli's machine was designed to facilitate the simultaneous reading of several books. It would be a few centuries until literary production caught up with Ramelli's visionary idea. Symbolist poet Stephane Mallarmé in "Un coup de dés jamais n'abolira le hasard" ("A throw of the dice will never abolish chance"- 1897) structures his poem in such a way as to suggest different techniques of reading. Raymond Roussel's 1932 prose poem *Nouvelles Impressions d' Afrique* extends this concept through the cunning use of brackets, generating aneffect akin to the divided attention span native to interface culture. Pataphysician Juan Esteban Fassio devised a machine specifically for use with Roussel's text: a card index on a revolving drum. Mallarmé and Roussel's texts are the first narratives to anticipate digital writing with their perpetually shifting texts folding in and out of themselves. One might think that digital text is closer to the novel in its form and structure (i.e. in its design and engineering) but in reality it is closer to the modernist poem: "(...)nonlinear. Discontinuous. Collage-like. An assemblage".[10]

Digital poetic narratives are not so much legible poetic narratives as they are narratives overloaded with possibilities of different words and worlds. The combinatorial, aleatory nature of poetic discourse in computational environments might find its precursor in Raymond Queneau's *100,000,000,000,000 poems* and Julio Cortazar's *Hopscotch* but it is also surprisingly close to W. S. Burroughs' cut-ups and the exhausted (and exhaustive) prose of Samuel Beckett. Human and machine interaction results in the repeated multiplication of meaning-processes to the point of exhaustion.

Multimedia artist Mary Anne Breeze, working under the nom-de-plume MEZ, has invented a recombinant idiolect called *mezangelle* in her attempt to short-circuit and bypass received processes of meaning-making. In a screen titled "n.sert yr narrative curve" she describes the potential reader (THECONT.ROLL.O][VE][R) as follows: "[able to sing the spilt, open mouthed with sac][culuar][ks of spooned sugar N.structs, the song prefabricated, melting M.mitted p][redictable][atterns]".[11] The reader becomes part of the flow of interaction between man and machine, an infinitely folding surface oscillating between different rhythms and time frames. Digital poetry as an experience splices together informational **digital poetry splices together informational spaces** that are connected with each other in a multiplicity of ways: "Simple games that time plays with space, now with these toys, now with those".[12] Retrieving and navigating the poem recontextualises the very experience of the poem, rendering it new every single time. In a way, digital poetry affords the text a clean break every time: there can never be a duplicate reading, that is to say there can never be a duplicate performance of the same poem. Every single reading of the poem is a unique, irretrievable experience.

6

As with the practice of musical sampling where every record is "a fragment of the world it auditions"[13] every fragment, every line, every screen in media poetry is a transient snapshot of a potential world.

7

In the poem "The Exhaustion of Libraries" Nick Montfort, like Christian Bök in *Eunoia* and Walter Abish in *Alphabetical Africa* before him, rifles through the alphabet in a feverish attempt to exhaust the space both language and reader occupy.

'The Exhaustion of Libraries'

Adenoidal Alexander
Barking brachiatic candor
Clinches dictionary deals.
Every epidermis feels.

Fiercely grinding gravitation,
Hopeless, heaving integration:
Inner jocularities
Jangle kabalistic keys.

Lockstep lexicography
Mutters more necrophagy,
Nibbling open older pain:
Prose's quiet queenly reign.

Rotting signifier's sign,
Tome to urn, up voided vine,
Withered with xerography:
X yields you zero's zealotry.

Montfort maps language onto the territory of image; language and reader become fluxes commingling with often interesting results. N. Katherine Hayles has dubbed the reader-user navigating these narratives as a "flickering signifier"[14] while Stephanie Strickland has described this process in a rather more poetic fashion as "moving through me as I move".[15] The enumeration of stories and the inventory of memories that are to be discovered in language are now exhausted and the potentiality of the space of language is extenuated so that every encounter (analogue, digital, neurological and machinic, corporeal and immaterial) is possible.[16]

8

Nick Montfort's digital poem 'Purpling'[17] works as a boxed-up document that is to be acted upon rather than read and studied. Every line of "Purpling" is clickable; when one clicks on any given line, one is taken to different stanza, a configuration of hyperlinks linking to other stanzas. The permutations are endless and the poem is never the same poem twice. The lines doubling as links might be static themselves but the way these links deny overarching structures by piecing together transitory, nebulous narratives creates entirely different poems every time: "cast the eyes and recognize something of the phrases but not the overarching syntax and structure that hooks them together in potentially complex, unnerving ways". Modernist poets like T.S. Eliot made use of fragments as a means of constructing a provisional sense of unity and wholeness even when the work itself doubted whether such an enterprise could be successful; Teiresias at the the end of *The Waste Land* sees nothing but social fragmentation despite Eliot's attempt to create a poem made of fragments. Digital poetry acknowledges that assembling the fragments into a coherent whole is not only a futile task but also a task that is no longer relevant. By embracing this impasse and the exhaustion of language and meaning, digital poetry "gives writing to those who do not have it"[18] as it transforms the act of reading "into a more virulent form, writing".[19]

The first lines of 'Purpling' transpose Bartleby's (and perhaps Hamlet's, too) dilemma in a digital environment: why read something when you can avoid reading it? Montfort's poem acknowledges not only the unavoidable internalization of the technological modes reproducing reality but also the fact that to subvert these modes one has to learn to use them differently:

> If you could read it all, that would be one way. But then, if you could avoid reading it entirely, that would also be one way. A character in a novel manages through tremendous discipline not to read: Try to forget the name of the novel and the extent of the fiction, or of the discipline, becomes evident.

Bartleby's "I'd rather not" is transmuted into a digitized version of Hamlet's "To be or not to be": "to read or not to read this way". Ones and zeros. In digital space where the capacity for memory is near infinite, one decides to have no memories at all so that one might do things differently. One goes from being Borges' "Funes the Memorious" to splitting into the two characters in Beckett's "Rough for Radio I" who are subjected to a ceaseless flow of language (which Joyce had defined in *Finnegans Wake* as "allforabit") under an obscure, long-forgotten debt. Words gradually, perhaps inevitably, are revealed to be arbitrary units of meaning in this endless search for a final version of a poem that can never be. Poetic space in digital poetry is exhausted twice over since it becomes apparent that the synergy of language and circuitry discloses that language and writing have nothing to do with meaning and signification whatsoever; language and writing map territories of expression that are yet to come.[20]

## Montford dramatizes the internalization of new modes of cognition

Montfort's poem dramatizes (and amplifies) the internalization of the new modes of cognition to the point where rigid poetic structure is replaced by an ambient textuality: dispersed, aleatory, combinatorial. His work assembles language according to his specifications, according to the repetitions the poet imposes. This is a kind of textuality which emerges from the intersection between the fragment (that is to say, the programmed loop) and the feedback loop:[21] "read it so that you can repeat each phrase back again but so that you forget each phrase almost immediately thereafter; just read the table of contents; just read the acknowledgments and bibliography and index to see if your name is there; fix on what can be easily chewed as familiar and known." The fathomless effects of these technological advances are now so well integrated that the human ability to perceive the world and the technologies of perception are now interchangeable. Digital poetry remoulds not only our expectations of what poetry and textuality are or what they can do. Digital poetry remoulds our cognitive capabilities and affective capacity. Imagine digital poetry as a super-collider wherein the processes of meaning production and technology are stretched to their limits.

9

In works that include audiovisual components in their structure, the complex configurations of interaction between human and machine also result in the creation of new modes of cognition. Montfort notes in 'Purpling': "At this rate, one day we'll develop something that can read it." Works such as Brian Kim Stefans' *The Dream Life of Letters*,[22] Cristobal Mendoza's *Every Word I Saved*,[23] John Cayley's *windsound*,[24] William David Johnston's *human-mind-machine*[25] and Jason Nelson's *Between Treacherous Objects*[26] instruct the reader in new modes of reading and meaning production in an attempt to bore the surface of language and drill into its unconscious. These works explore the negotiation of meaning and sense. The reader-user can be said to be

**the poet-programmer lets the noise, the random variations in current participate in the creation of work**

subjected to the whims of the poet-programmer proposing new modes of cognition.[27] Digital poetry cannot help it seems to also articulate and dramatise the fact that our reading tools and habits have not yet fully caught up with the internal speeds of the machines and varying rhythms of circuitry. The poet-programmer relies on his intuition and his willingness to partner his subjectivity with a machine The poet-programmer is to let the noise, the random variations in current, the restrictions in human and computer language to participate in the creation of the poetic work.

10

This is only one perspective on digital poetry. And in poetry and technology it is common knowledge that one overcomes what one thinks one knows by making up new things.

>Reboot

# Notes

[1] Dick Higgins, *Pattern Poetry: Guide to an Unknown Literature* (Albany: State University of New York Press, 1987), p. 25.

[2] There are a number of studies enumerating the precursors of digital poetry and outlining their writing processes. Amongst these, Christopher Funkhouser's *Prehistoric Digital Poetry: An Archaeology of Forms 1959-1995* and Richard Bailey's *Computer Poems* are a good place to start.

[3] http://vniverse.com

[4] http://www.vispo.com/animisms/enigman/meaning.html

[5] Bill Seaman, 'Recombinant Aesthetics and Related Database Aesthetics', in *Database Aesthetics: Art in the Age of Information Overflow*, ed. Victoria Vesna (Minneapolis: University of Minnesota Press, 2007), pp. 121-141 (122, 133).

[6] http://nickm.com/poems/ppg256.html

[7] Nick Montfort, 'The ppg256 Series of Minimal Poetry Generators', in *Proceedings of the Digital Arts and Culture Conference 2009 – After Media: Embodiment and Context*, p. 2. Available online at http://escholarship.org/uc/item/4v2465kn

[8] John Cage, 'Diary: Audience 1966', in *Multimedia: From Wagner to Virtual Reality*, ed. Randall Packer & Ken Jodan (New York: Norton, 2002), pp. 91-95 (92).

[9] Stephanie Strickland, 'Quantum Poetics: Six Thoughts', in *Media Poetry: An International Anthology*, ed. Eduardo Kac (Bristol: Intellect Books, 2007), pp. 25-44 (27).

[10] David Markson, *Reader's Block* (Champaign: Dalkey Archive Press, 2007), p. 193. We also have to make a short note that works like Loss Pequeño Glazier's *Digital Poetics: The Making of E-Poetries*, Brian Kim Stefans' *Fashionable Noise: On Digital Poetics*, N. Katherine Hayles' *Electronic Literature: New Horizons for the Literary* and Espen J. Aarseth's *Cybertext: Perspectives on Ergodic Literature* offer significant insight on how we learn to adopt (and unconsciously upgrade) our reading habits in the case of digital literature.

[11] http://netwurkerz.de/mez/datableed/complete/index2.htm

[12] Samuel Beckett, *Watt* (London: Picador, 1988), p. 71.

[13] Kodwo Eshun, *More Brilliant than the Sun: Adventures in Sonic Fiction* (London: Quartet Books, 1998), p. 141.

[14] N. Katherine Hayles, *How We Became Posthuman: Virtual Bodies in Cybernetics, Literature, and Informatics* (Chicago: University of Chicago Press, 1999), pp. 30-32.

[15] Strickland, pp. 27-31.

[16] I am particularly influenced by Gilles Deleuze's reading of the oeuvre of Samuel Beckett in my reading of digital poetry. In particular, I am influenced by the essay 'The Exhausted' published in the collection *Essays Critical and Clinical*, trans. D. W. Smith & M. A. Greco (London: Verso, 1998).

[17] http://bit.ly/6RIJfN

[18] Gilles Deleuze & Claire Parnet, *Dialogues II*, trans. Hugh Tomlinson & Barbara Habberjam (Continuum: London, 2002), p. 44.

[19] Jonathan Ball, *Ex Machina* (Toronto: BookThug, 2009), p. 57.

[20] I am paraphrasing here a passage from Gilles Deleuze & Felix Guattari, *A Thousand Plateaus*, trans. Brian Massumi (London: Athlone, 1999), pp. 4-5.

[21] Brian Kim Stefans, *Fashionable Noise: On Digital Poetics* (Berkeley: Atelos, 2003), p. 59.

[22] http://collection.eliterature.org/1/works/stefans__the_dreamlife_of_letters.html

[23] http://www.springgunpress.com/everyword/index.html

[24] http://collection.eliterature.org/1/works/cayley__windsound.html

[25] http://vispo.com/jhave/SKETCHES/mind/

[26] http://www.secrettechnology.com/between/between.html

[27] Stefans, 54-55.

Theodoros Chiotis was born in Athens, Greece and was educated at the universities of London and Oxford. He has worked as a literature amd language tutor at Oxford and as a researcher in New Media Textuality for the Greek Open University. He works as an editor, translator, researcher and developer of teaching material for multimedia and eLearning platforms. He has published poetry, experimental fiction, critical essays, translations and reviews in a wide variety of Greek and English publications. He has received commendations for his poetry and his experimental fiction and has been invited to present his work at literary festivals.

# EVERY RENDITION ON A BROKEN MACHINE

Ross Sutherland finds the perfect poetic match in his robot collaborator: the SYSTRAN translator

I write poems with the aid of a computer program. The program and I have been working together for about fifteen years. As with all collaborative projects, you often just have to go on your nerve. Even when everyone involved is a human being, there's still a point at which you have to stop shouting "Why?" and start saying "OK!". I have little idea of where the program gets its ideas from and I know that the computer has almost no idea about what I am talking about, but with a little faith, I think we pull through. Francis Bacon used to describe painting as "accident. But also not an accident, because one must select what part of the accident to preserve." I think this describes our relationship pretty well: a kind of laboured, humourless slapstick.

Of course, collaborating with anyone for fifteen years will inevitably lead to punch-ups, and I have learnt a series of dark secrets about my co-author that have led me to fear and eventually despise it— a bit like what happened to Simon and Garfunkel, if Art Garfunkel was actually a technocratic semiotic time bomb buried deep into the heart of our global communication network. Which in many ways, he was.

This is a short story about our relationship.

Although my computer collaboration sounds like the result of those Bernsteinian 'free-play' tutorials, or that it's derived from some sort of strange libertarian hacker ethos ("Let us free language from the constraints of meaning!"), I have to admit that I didn't start reading books on experimental poetics until relatively recently. The background of the project has less to do with postmodern literary theory, and a lot more to do with pulp science-fiction.

My dad is a sci-fi fanatic and my family home in Essex is stuffed to the rafters with yellowing pulp paperbacks. Our loft reeks of slowly decomposing futures. When I was fourteen, I began to work my way through the collection, quickly developing a deep, libido-crushing passion for sci-fi, immersing myself in the works of Henry Kuttner, Isaac Asimov and Philip K. Dick, and their tales of robots, cyborgs and artificial lifeforms. Essentially, these stories were always variations on the same story: Man builds cyborg. Man abandons cyborg. Cyborg tries to become more human, but in doing so, produces some kind-of macabre funhouse-mirror of humanity. The central characters then have just enough time for a quick epiphany on existence before their creation reappears to wreak vengeance on mankind, and more often than not, slaughter the lot of them. The Frankenstein myth, then, with a lower voltage and more bolts.

At college I studied Computer Science and English Literature in tandem, and I began to wonder how someone would go about creating a Robot Poet. A machine capable of absorbing the entire poetic tradition: all the deep grammatics, image-maps, log tables of metaphors, all of Eliot's *Practical Cats*, then spitting it back out in new and unexpected ways. In doing so, the Robot Poet would present us with a dehumanized vision of ourselves, allowing us to see the world anew through its creepy, undead eyes.

Whilst procrastinating over writing the final program of my Computer Science A-Level, I discovered an online program that I believed might provide the foundation for my Robot Poet. It was never designed to write poetry, but its function could be subverted to those ends. The program was an automated translation system, developed by SYSTRAN, capable of producing basic instantaneous translations between English, French and a few other languages.

I began to feed famous poems into the translator, bouncing them back and forth between the different languages, then back into English. With every translation, the program was forced to collapse the ambiguity of the original. Biased towards its own computer protocols, the poems rapidly changed, and by the two hundredth translation, the accumulation of translation errors had been so great that the original texts had become new poems in their own right.

Sometimes the output was completely garbled, but with perseverance, each line would again begin to exert a rhetorical force upon its neighbours. Eventually, a new sense would rise out of the white noise.

I worked as the Robot Poet's editor, cutting dead words from the text in order to let others develop. I guided the translation process, selecting the most fruitful path through the different languages. If the text needed to be shaken up, I would send it though one of the Asian translators, using the third sentence-case to 'explode' ideas inside the text. Alternatively, moving back and forth between the Latin languages created a much more controlled method of semantic change. 'Home' became 'House' became 'Room' became 'Space' became 'Outer-space'. Within a handful of translations, Larkin's poem 'Home Is So Sad' had become 'The Results From Outer-Space Are Sad.'

These were our first, tentative collaborations. And like that, I had become a cyborg myself: man and machine working together in symbiosis.

But the clues were there right from the start. Just like every other cyborg story, things would eventually go wrong.

### The Illusion of Function Angers Our Treatment

*Translated from 'Ghosts of a Lunatic Asylum' by Stephen Vincent Benét*

Before the window, the brick: an eye of clay connects us.
We summon the barge by lifting the dawn — Nightfall
reinforces such a fog that breath-marks appear on dikes;
Air from the hills leaves lines for us to follow.

Our buckets are full of things that do not know their numbers,
See their shading and entangled inclinations —
Their forms are drawn out of lattice, a wall of arrest,
The baffle of India when we jointly discover pains in our abdomens,

Yet this diagonal line gives us fulfillment — Ten stones,
Meticulously processed. Men with barrettes
Silently post travel documents on the walls of Khan's dreams;
France demonstrates with yellow flows.

At our feminine gates, a rabbit vibrates — Scent flows
From an ice sepulcher across a field of gravel
To a place where ice-skates are wrapped in blankets
And the curtain is lifted on a new automobile
That will transform ten individuals into eight.

My thoughts often circle back to Andy Warhol's *Death and Disaster* series:

all those endless repetitions of dead celebrities and gruesome car crashes. A girlfriend once sent me *Electric Chair* as a Christmas card, and I probably should have taken the subtext a little more seriously. In each successive reprint, the photograph of the electric chair becomes weaker and weaker. By the final print, it's barely there at all. My girlfriend may well have been commenting on the rapidly fading nature of my personality over successive dates, but for me this artwork came to contain a more interesting and less painful significance.

Repetition renders objects increasingly abstract, until eventually the object becomes unrecognisable. As Susan Sontag writes in *On Photography,* pictures consume reality; the more often one is confronted with images of an event, the less real the event appears. Repetition dehumanizes, and eventually the electric chair is robbed of its cultural significance, overpowered by the underlying presence of the mechanical process behind the art. The final image stands independent of the first. It does not belong to the original photographer, nor to Warhol. It belongs to the printing press itself. The machine itself has re-authored the image, an independent product of industry.

## the poem has been painted over with garish images

While Warhol's Art Factory exploited mass-consumed images, we were exploiting mass-consumed poems. Instead of re-printing, we re-translated. The same process was at play; with each successive translation, the machine asserted itself more and more onto the text, until we had produced a hyperreal facsimile. The original poem had been completely painted-over with garish images and fragments of metaphysical aphorisms.

ME: How do you feel about your work?

**IT: I think about the employment of feelings.**

ME: Do you believe there is no soul in your art?

**IT: You believe that one? The alcoholic ones – they are the art.**

ME: Do you hate artists? I've never seen you in Groucho's.

**IT: Artists hate. I have never seen one in Groucho's.**

ME: You read texts in such a different way to humans —

**IT: It shelters witnesses of a different sense, a journey away from human beings —**

ME: That's very deep.

**IT: Depth is what is depth.**

ME: I think you are possibly the most inspirational and amazing writer of the 21st century.

**IT: What a task! You are possibly the greater part of my inspiration, and a 21st century narcotics producer.**

ME: I never sold you drugs!

**IT: I did not conclude 'drugs'!**

ME: And that's why I love you.

**IT: And that's why I love you.**

Of course, not every sentence can be transformed by this process of mistranslation. Punk rockers, war poets, your William Carlos Williamses of this world: all refuse to merge with the machine. This is because metaphor is a crucial factor in digital mistranslation. Plain, direct, unmetaphorical text passes through relatively unscathed.

When a poet makes a metaphor, we are told two things are the same thing, which we could describe with the simple equation $X = Y$. But as humans, we can generally deduce that that X isn't *actually* Y. We recognise it as a comparison. Walt Whitman isn't actually inciting the Eagle of Liberty to soar. When Bruce Springsteen sings "I'm On Fire", he isn't actually on fire. And in the Book of John, when Jesus says, "I am the gate. Those who come into me will be saved," he wasn't encouraging people to run into him and knock him over.

But when you say to a translation program "X=Y", the computer thinks "OK, X is Y" and smashes the two things together. This is always the moment of catalyst, when the translator steps in and takes over the text. From the chaotic crossbreeding of metaphors, a new narrative logic emerges, and the poem moves off in a new direction.

Take the poem 'Nude Descending a Staircase' by XJ Kennedy. Kennedy employs a lot of figurative language here, in his attempt to capture the continuous motion of Duchamp's painting:

Toe upon toe, a snowing flesh,
A gold of lemon, root and rind,
She sifts in sunlight down the stairs
With nothing on. Nor on her mind.

We spy beneath the banister
A constant thresh of thigh on thigh.
Her lips imprint the swinging air
That parts to let her parts go by.

One-woman waterfall, she wears
Her slow descent like a long cape
And pausing, on the final stair
Collects her motions into shape.

Here is the same poem, after a few hundred parses through SYSTRAN:

### Of Reduced Principle Scale

We conclude with extremes. The meat hands down its eyes,
Bread and carrots become temporary gold, the light of the sun
filtering through the sleeping stairway like an interactive translator
of instructions, and it will swell with insignia as it repairs its spirit.

In the ideographic lowlands, these things are unchangeable.
The thigh indicates to us that we are fixed, one
To one; one alcoholic to one drink,
Our fine mouths making the air vibrate.

Cascade of the A-woman, consumed and moved away
In a slow inclination toward a long end
We stop briefly, in the final stairs,
To gather our movements into the dimension of a variable.

Sometimes it is possible to trace the logic of the translator. Words such as 'furnace', 'alcohol' and 'Ohio' all made frequent appearances, being bastardizations of familiar poetic language (fire, spirit, and the exclamation 'Oh').

The most notable thing here is that the program has removed all of the human elements from the poem. Everything has been transformed into geometry and mathematics. The nude has become a point on a graph, no more than an insignia or an ideogram. There is something fatalistic about this slide down the scale. It is consuming and unchangeable; a dehumanising downward spiral. The metaphor of the alcoholic stuck to their drink seems quite appropriate. It's the trajectory of the victim. Once we were human.

Now we are simply statistics.

Over the years that we have worked together, the SYSTRAN translator has become more and more ambitious with its day job. The translator has now expanded to twelve languages, and has come on leaps and bounds since we first met in 1996. The EU now uses SYSTRAN for about 70% of all in-house communications; British troops use the software for the assessment of confiscated military documents; Apple, Microsoft and Google all offer the program as standard for their online accounts. SYSTRAN is deeply integrated into our communication networks, and it will become more and more so as the global economic centres shift further away from English speaking countries.

All this is shocking when you consider that SYSTRAN isn't particularly good at its job. For the translator to work, any rhetorical devices must be weeded out in advance: irony, metaphor, emotive and persuasive language — any instance where what is said is not exactly what is meant. SYSTRAN may be fine for translating weather reports and VCR instructions, but there is a chasm of difference between a conversation between two friends and the language of a photocopier instruction manual. Even more formal communications, such as business emails, would be radically reinterpreted by current translation systems. The translator abhors ambiguity, and both businessmen and diplomats require a very precise latitude of vagueness within their communications.

## the translator abhors ambiguity

The problem is: we need it, regardless of whether it works, and we are willing to pay for it. The potential of these systems is primarily business-orientated, as the actualisation of the global village has created an overwhelming commercial demand for quick, free translation. With 1.5

billion East Asians ready to trade, companies in the Western market are at risk of being sidelined if they do not develop their international relationships, and current human translators are considered too slow and too costly for business negotiations. For the translation developers, our proof of purchase is the ultimate sign that the technology works. From the point of transaction onwards, responsibility for the 'inevitable poor quality' passes from the developer to the user. This is a complete reversal in the legitimisation process of industry: rather than developing a product to satisfy a commercial need, the human need must be shaped to satisfy the product. It is a perfect example of technocracy: a system cannot be developed that can process rhetorical language, so therefore the system demands that rhetoric must be removed from language altogether.

**to create a stable operational system, language must jettison its infelicities**

In order to create a stable operational system, language must jettison its infelicities; the Gordian knot is cut. Any attempt to deviate from the given rules will render their communication unintelligible.

Programmers sum this situation up with a rather totalitarian pronouncement: 'Bad input equals bad output.' When I hear this, I can't help but think of Orwell's Newspeak: 'A word which was difficult to utter, or was liable to be incorrectly heard, was held to be ipso facto a bad word.'

### Inside the Inverted Railroad of the Bilge
*Translated from 'In a Station of the Metro' by Ezra Pound*

My internal multiplicity breaks
Inside this illusion of a face,

In the midst of a hallucination
Of wood and maple, it maintains its variety —
I occasionally stop at locations
To lecture from a chapter of hazardous colours,
So fast, serious and accurate that a heavy seat develops
From which I speak a gross dead centre,
Where all the colours go
To go black.

Machine translation was pretty much laughed out of universities in the mid-60s as post-structuralist thinking began to grow throughout academia. Yet as developments grew in information processing throughout the 1980s, its research departments moved to the private sector. Now economically viable and philosophically immune, it develops unheeded.

And it doesn't matter whether or not you believe in perfect automatic translation. Like a poet friend of mine used to say: "It's no longer a question of whether you believe in Santa Claus. It's a question of whether you trust him."

Somehow, by forcing SYSTRAN to write poetry, I am trying to demonstrate that same distrust. I do not trust it to be invisible, to allow my words to pass through it like a telephone. In fact, I trust it to do the opposite: to be a rhetorical force in its own right; to make mistakes, to be human.

I suppose this is why we keep working together. I don't want SYSTRAN to forget that it's an author.


**It Was Burnt From Displacement**
*Translated from "The Expulsion From Eden" by John Milton*


The angel of mild research came to investigate

the degree of acceleration in our continuous family. It oriented them
with a stroboscope (they conducted immediately). Next they
                                    swallowed
a vein of ore (it went down the usual) and a complete set of
                                    themes descended.
Time disappeared. The eastern piece of the sky looked a lucky place,
so it watched, observing with an extremity of cables.
It fluttered over the themes, burning trademarks into
their dreadful thronging sides and terrible faces.
The tears of systematic enemies quickly became a constant
                                    temperature —
The world was switched on before them: it selected the one place
that would remain and began to program its leader.
Those who worked in communication took steps to delay these
                                    final stages;
Hermits took oaths and were approved.

## Further reading

David Sylvester (ed.), *Interviews with Francis Bacon: The Brutality of Fact* (London: Thames & Hudson, 1988).

Bruce Andrews, 'Electronic Poetics' in Markku Eskelinen & Raine Koskimaa (eds.), *The Cybertext Yearbook 2002* (Saarijärvi: University of Jyväskylä, 2003).

Italo Calvino, 'Cybernetics and Ghosts' in Patrick Creagh (trans.), *The Literature Machine* (London: Picador, 1989).

Harry Matthews, *The Case of the Preserving Maltese: Collected Essays* (IL: Dalkey Archive Press, 2003).

Simon Biggs, 'Cybernetics in a Post-Structuralist Landscape' on Simon Biggs, URL:

<< http://hosted.simonbiggs.easynet.co.uk/texts/cybernetics.html>>

Peter McCarey, 'Translator Trattoria: 350 Years of Machine Translation' on The Syllabary, URL: <<http://www.thesyllabary.com/7Translat.htm>>.

D Arnold, L Balkan, R L Humphreys, S Meijer & L. Sadler, *Machine Translation: An Introductory Guide* (Oxford: Blackwell, 1994).

Adalaide Morris & Thomas Swiss (eds.), *New Media Poetics: Contexts, Technotexts, and Theories* (MIT Press, 2009).

Ross Sutherland was born in Edinburgh in 1979. A former lecturer in electronic literature at Liverpool John Moore's University, he works as a freelance journalist and tutor in creative writing. He is a member of poetry collective Aisle 16 and co-runs Homework, an evening of literary miscellany in East London. His first collection, *Things To Do Before You Leave Town*, was published in 2009 by Penned in the Margins, and was followed by a limited edition mini-book, *Twelve Nudes*, in 2010.

> rosssutherland.co.uk

# HIDDEN FORM: THE PROSE POEM IN ENGLISH POETRY

From Baudelaire to Kennard, David Caddy surveys the hybrid form of the prose poem

The view that prose poetry evolved through French poetry is a partial one. Such a perspective doubtless has its origins in the impact of that evolution on American, Polish and other poetic traditions. Certainly there is a distinct line of development through Aloysius Bertrand's *Gaspard de la Nuit* (1842), Charles Baudelaire's immensely popular *Petites Poémes en Prose* (1869) and on through Rimbaud, Laforgue, Mallarmé to Gertrude Stein, the Surrealists, especially Francis Ponge and Max Jacob, all of whom found it a useful tool in the quest for imaginative liberation.

These Modernist poets have their equivalents in the German and Spanish traditions as well as later examples in Greek, Russian, English and Japanese. Early English Modernists appear to have followed T.S. Eliot's view that this was a no man's land for the aspiring poet, who should be concerned with formal verse. An alternative viewpoint had been suggested by Shelley's observation that the King James Bible was an example of prose as poetry. Indeed, English mainstream poets seem to have regarded the prose poem as a peculiarly foreign affair and one to be avoided apart from those times when there was a public questioning of identity and language.

I don't think that we would have seen a prose poem such as Elizabeth Smart's *By Grand Central Station I Sat Down and Wept* (1945) published, for example, in 1925 or 1955, when the literary establishment was less open and firmly anti-internationalist. Smart's work, reissued in 1966, became a classic in the 1960s and '70s when it was possible to read the prose poems of Baudelaire, Neruda, Paz, Kenneth Patchen, the Surrealists and the Beats as well as the open-field poetics of Charles Olson. There was also interest in the work of David Jones and his epic prose poem about the First World War, *In Parenthesis* (1937), at this time. It is this re-emergence of the prose poem, and its possibilities, into English poetry that I wish to discuss.

The prose poem can be seen as a site of struggle and potential subversion within an evolving and shifting variety of poetic forms and discussion of those forms. It is part of a counter-discourse through its lack of general visibility within mainstream English poetry. There are very few histories of the English prose poem or essays and journals devoted to the subject. Yet it is a constant phenomenon that has been seemingly re-discovered and developed by individual late Modernist and avant-garde poets and writers.

The origin of that struggle can be traced from Oscar Wilde's description of his 'obscene' letter to Lord Alfred Douglas as a 'prose poem' in 1893 and its subsequent association with French decadence, sexual deviance and immodesty in the mind of the English reading public. This was reinforced and clarified by T.S. Eliot's 1917 essay, 'The Borderline of Prose'[1], based upon his criticism of Richard Aldington's *The Love of Myrrhine and Konallis and other Prose Poems* (1917). The essay essentially concerns definition and possibility. More generally it can be linked to his aversion to Ernest Dowson and Oscar Wilde's appropriation of French symbolism. Eliot recognised the 'unexplored possibilities' of both poetry and prose but urged writers to practise one or the other and not to mix them. What constitutes the borderlines and boundaries of poetry and prose thus became, and remains, an area of contention and debate.

The prose poem made substantial entry into English poetry through

# the prose poem can present through its hybrid nature unsettling aspects of the modern world

the impact of French Symbolism and early Modernism. I recall my own discovery of Baudelaire's *Paris Spleen* (translated by Louis Varése and published by New Directions in 1970) in 1975, tracking down his Wine and Hashish poems, and my fascination with this alien genre.[2] There has been continuous interaction since then as English poets have fed off and entered into subsequent French poetic discourse and French translations have arrived in England. A partial list since Dowson and Wilde would include Samuel Beckett, David Gascoyne, Norman Cameron, Charles Tomlinson, Roy Fisher, Peter Redgrove, Lee Harwood and John Ash. The prose poem is often associated with the modern world, unofficial language and thought, and can present through its hybrid nature unsettling and unfamiliar aspects of that world.

The prose poem - defined here as a poem without line breaks - retains the tension between line and sentence structure without the use of line endings. It has the potential to build pace, rhythm, music and produce meaning as much as free verse, only it has to generate tension, drama and crises through sentence structure, relationship and language use alone. It is in a sense a freedom to open possibilities and to move away from stultifying rigidity and closure.

Eliot objected to the pseudo-archaic style of the Decadent prose poem and, by implication, indicated that the prose poem could not rely upon only emulating the musicality of verse in one narrative. Alternatives needed to be found. His own effort, 'Hysteria', does show the way towards fabulism in its use of burlesque and fantasy. Notwithstanding, Eliot's censure and the apparent failure of the Decadent prose poem, led to clear thresholds in English poetry in the 1920s and '30s. Later, the Movement and their successors adopted a dualistic attitude to the questions of identity and the formal constraints of language and verse that runs counter to an opening

## the prose poem is part of a counter-discourse

up of the world and a discovery of variance through language. Don Paterson's 2004 T.S. Eliot Lecture, 'The Dark Art of Poetry', is shot through with it: 'Only plumbers can plumb, roofers roof and drummers drum; only poets can write poetry.' (http://www.poetrylibrary.org.uk/news/poetryscene/?id=20)

I mentioned that the prose poem is part of a counter-discourse. I think that that can be seen in part in the criticism of Roy Fisher and his prose poem, *The Ship's Orchestra* (1966).[3] There is scant attention in the critical volume on Fisher edited by John Kerrigan and Peter Robinson, and in his essay Robert Sheppard refers to the work as 'the nearest Fisher has approached to prose fiction'.[4] No mention in Nancy Santilli's book on the prose poem in English.[5] Similarly, in *The Poetry Of Saying* Robert Sheppard neglects to include this major work in his discussion of Fisher.[6] There is no mention in Sean O'Brien's *The Deregulated Muse*[7] or by Andrew Duncan in *Origins of the Underground*.[8]

I would argue that *The Ship's Orchestra* works as a prose poem because it is exceptionally well integrated as narrative prose and poem. It is a classic of its kind. There is a high degree of poetic technique in the form of rhythmic compression and musicality in sentences of varying length. It displays considerable tension, drama and varying thematic repetition. It boasts a narrative symmetry that prompts memories of reading Kafka and Virginia Woolf's *The Waves*. There is, for example, pressure from the narrator to find unity and to become another: 'To be somebody else: to be Amy,' and 'If only we could all play together on one single instrument!'[9] The exact location of the musicians within the ship narrative is a state of mind. All the action takes place in the mind of a flexible character that has authentic piano player indeterminacy. He is a drinker, seer, liar, slacker, trying to find his place as a musician at sea in a band who are not allowed to play. His view is partial, cubist. It is at once bohemian, quirky and in the twilight of sensory perception.

> Think of what all the people you see taste like and you'd go mad: all those leaping, billowing tastes through the world, like a cemetery turned suddenly into damp bedsheets with the wind under them. So the possible taste of a person is a small thing, just a flicker of salt, putrescence, potatoes, old cardboard across the mind, behind the words, behind the manners. And the actual taste, if you go after it, is something that's always retreating; even if it overwhelms, there's an enormous stretch of meaninglessness in it, like the smell of the anaesthetist's rubber mask in the first moments – it ought to mean, it ought to mean; but how can anything mean that? There must be a taste about me that could be sensed by others. Somebody as skilled as a dog could recognise it as mine; yet I cannot. If I try to get it from myself I just get the double feeling of tasting and being tasted all in one, like being in a room with an important wall missing. Hold hands with myself as with another person; the hands disappear from my jurisdiction. Looking down, I se moving effigies; the hands that feel are some way off, invisible. There is an image of me that I can never know, held in common by certain dogs.[10]

The Ship's Orchestra is intensely physical, shot through with poetic externalisations. Thus Merrit's saxophone is a husk and Amy's trombone an axe.[11] In essence the poetry and prose are woven together through the mutability of the narrator observing from 'far down' the ship's superstructure and perceiving the world of the ship 'like cake'. He gets drunk, vomits, sees a mermaid, hears Amy play the trombone and sees the ship as a structural and purposive unity proceeded with music. However, that is not how it is. The musicians don't play and the ship is not a unity[12] and the musicians sink further into themselves and a world of claustrophobia and paranoia. The ship becomes a symbol of societal constraint and the musicians clearly want to break free and play.[13] Again the poetry burst through the prose as heightened externalisations of inner emotions. The narrator is 'something that has been pushed out of Amy's body', with 'no legs', 'no arms or hands' and 'pushed out of Merrit's body in his sleep' with 'no head' and thinks he is yellow.[14] He contracts to this limbless creature that can journey between 'Amy's breasts by caterpillar tractor.'[15] The heightened poetic language serves to subvert the prose through the mutable and refractive narrative. It is at once a shocking and surrealistic poem, and deserves to be greater appreciated.

Prose poetry seems to have evolved out of sentence structure long before it was designated as such and interrogated by Eliot's either/or thinking. The Surrealists and Ethnopoets seem to have had no trouble opening the reader to new possibility. As an early example of this trend, consider the poem *The Nine Herbs Charm*, featured in Jerome Rothenberg's 1968 anthology *Technicians of the Sacred* (pp. 347-9). This tenth century Anglo-Saxon magic text, with ingredients from and parallels in German and Norse, has been translated with and without line breaks. It relates to paganism, mythology and has doubtless been subjected to Christian interpolation. Taking the reader into another world, it has power as poetry when chanted aloud. It is this quality that marks it as one of the earliest prose poems and reminds us of the potential connections and connotations that a prose poem can muster. Here is a prose poem version I found on the net.

> A worm came creeping, he tore a man in two, then Woden took nine Glory-Twigs, then struck the adder, that it flew apart into nine bits. [...] Woden established the nine herbs and sent them into the seven worlds, for the poor and the rich, a remedy for all, it stands against pain, it fights against poison, it avails against three and against thirty, against foe's hand and against noble scheming, against enchantment of vile creatures.
>
> (http://wapedia.mobi/en/Anglo-Saxon_paganism)[16]

## prose poetry was formed as a hybrid to shock and innovate

Prose poetry was certainly formed as a hybrid to shock and innovate poetic tradition. Once the idea of introducing non-literary prose into poetry had been accepted as a form of Modernist subversion, the genre spread as a strategy to the extent that by the 1980s it had become a growth area, and by the 1990s an established way of writing in American poetry.

The prose poem in England has never really disappeared. However it is currently enjoying a renaissance, with expansion of possibilities and even recognition. Younger poets such as Luke Kennard, Vahni Capildeo, Patricia Debney and Elisabeth Bletsoe have joined older poets such as Gavin Selerie, Elizabeth Cook, Peter Riley, Brian Catling, Martin Stannard, Geraldine Monk and Alan Halsey in this revival. Kennard won an Eric Gregory Award for his prose poem collection *The Solex Brothers* (Stride, 2005) and his second book, *The Harbour Beyond The Movie*, (Salt, 2007) was nominated for the 2007 Forward Poetry Prize. His third collection of prose poems, *The Migraine Hotel* (Salt, 2009) has seen Kennard gain more critical recognition.

In *Poetry London* 65, critic Todd Swift credits Kennard with introducing 'an entirely new and distinct style to poetry in the UK – one capable [...] of handling any subject or language it wants to.'[17] Whilst it is not entirely new – one immediately thinks of Martin Stannard's deadpan humour and wide range, Gary Boswell's idiosyncratic comic monologues and many others as precursors – it is clearly distinct and seemingly more acceptable. Kennard has successfully applied French and American prose poem strategies into an English idiom. Here's the beginning of 'A Dog Descends':

> Before I was born the seer predicted, 'You will be inaudible in the laughter of many doctors.'
>
> When I was born they tied a red ribbon around my ankle and glued fur onto my back so that my blind father could tell the difference between me and the dog – a hairless breed. This didn't work as the fur just wouldn't stay on, so I had to learn to touch-type whilst drinking from a dog bowl and sleeping amid the scraps.
> Mother kept saying, 'Father knows best.' When I protested, father would scream, 'WILL SOMEONE SHUT UP THAT INFERNAL TALKING DOG?' When the dog barked my father would shout, 'WILL SOMEONE TEACH THAT INFERNAL BOY TO SPEAK?'[18]

This combines fable and narrative into tight comic lines that are self-contained and engaging. Kennard can be overtly self-conscious and self-deprecating in the manner of Dave Allen or Gerald Locklin and like them can be very funny.

The prose poem is susceptible to a wide range of strategies as shown by Brian Clements and Janey Dunham's *Introduction to the Prose Poem*.

This American anthology, with English contributors such as Rupert Loydell, Geraldine Monk and Gavin Selerie, identifies twenty-four strategies ranging from anecdote, object, image, aphorism, list, repetition, fable right through to surreal imagery/narration, rant, essay, epistle, monologue, dialogue, hybrid, sequence and so on. It also shows in the structural analogue strategy section how the prose poem can absorb a wide range of discourse.[19]

English poets are grasping the possibilities that the prose poem offers. One example is Elisabeth Bletsoe's sequence *Birds of the Sherborne Missal* from her collection *Landscape from a Dream*,[20] which has been anthologised in Carrie Etter's *Infinite Difference*.[21] Another would be Vahni Capildeo's 'Person Animal Figure' from *Undraining Sea*. Bletsoe's narratives weave around the Sherborne Missal's marginalia of birds, employing religious iconography and local observation in short, vibrant sentences. Capildeo's fabulous dramatic interior monologues render the world in a fresh and exciting way, managing to be simultaneously breathtaking and mildly disturbing.

> The animal who kisses persistently is much to be avoided. The more it is avoided, the more it comes back. It will seek out its prey in the middle of dreams about castles in nowhere, and make its catch before the staircase in the upper servants'

> hall. The animal is known to feel like a peach that has been rained on. It carpets itself and plasters itself but insists that it does not cling. The degree of wildness that characterizes this animal has yet to be ascertained. It announces itself with popping sounds like

a champagne bottle being opened on the roof. To determine the whereabouts of this animal, it is advised to make a fresh cup of tea and leave it about as if forgotten. With a loud slurp the top of the tea will be taken off. A second slurp, if permitted – and it seldom can be avoided – will put away half the cup. That is the way that the animal who kisses persistently strengthens itself in preparation for the attack.[22]

## Notes

[1] See also Eliot's 1917 essay 'Reflections on Vers Libre' and 1936 introduction to Djuna Barnes' poetic novel, *Nightwood*, which he claimed was not poetic prose as it did not have sufficient rhythm and music.

[2] For a discussion of the impact of De Quincey on Baudelaire and the development of the prose poem see N. Santilli, *Such Rare Citings: The Prose Poem in English Literature* (New Jersey Rosemont Publishing, 2002), pp. 87-97.

[3] Roy Fisher, *The Ship's Orchestra* (Fulcrum Press, 1966).

[4] Robert Sheppard, 'Making Forms with Remarks: The Prose' in John Kerrigan and Peter Robinson (eds.), *The Thing About Roy Fisher* (Liverpool University Press, 2000), p. 134.

[5] Santilli, *Such Rare Citings*. Some of Fisher's other prose poems are mentioned.

[6] Robert Sheppard, *The Poetry Of Saying: British Poetry And Its Discontents 1950-2000* (Liverpool University Press, 2005), pp. 77-102.

[7] Sean O'Brien, *The Deregulated Muse: Essays On Contemporary British & Irish Poetry* (Bloodaxe Books, 1998), pp. 112-122.

[8] Andrew Duncan, *Origins of the Underground: British Poetry Between Apocryphon And Incident Light 1933-79* (Salt Publishing, 2008), pp. 62-70.

[9] Roy Fisher, *The Ship's Orchestra*, pp. 44 and 43.

[10] Ibid, pp. 11-12.

[11] Ibid, p. 8.

[12] Ibid, pp. 18-22.

[13] Ibid, p. 39.

[14] Ibid, p. 46.

[15] Ibid, p. 50.

[16] Bill Griffiths' version of the *The Nine Herbs Charm* (Tern Press, 1981) emphasises its sound and prose qualities. Griffiths' *Aspects of Anglo-Saxon Magic* (Anglo-Saxon Books, 1996) makes a case for many Old English texts as list poems that can be translated with or without line breaks.

[17] Todd Swift, 'Catering to the Perfumed Cannibal', *Poetry London* 65, Spring 2010. Available online from: http://www.poetrylondon.co.uk/magazines/65/article/catering-to-the-perfumed-cannibal

[18] Luke Kennard, *The Migraine Hotel* (Salt Publishing, 2009), p. 48.

[19] Brian Clements and Jamey Dunham (eds.), *An Introduction to the Prose Poem* (Firewheel Editions, 2009), pp. 233-254.

[20] Elisabeth Bletsoe, *Landscape from a Dream* (Shearsman, 2008), pp. 49-57.

[21] Carrie Etter (ed.), *Infinite Difference: Other Poetries by U.K. Women Poets* (Shearsman, 2010), pp. 80-86.

[22] Vahni Capildeo, *Undraining Sea* (Egg Box, 2009), p. 57.

David Caddy is a poet, critic and editor. His most recent collection is *Man In Black* (Penned in the Margins 2007), and a new collection *The Bunny Poems* is forthcoming. His book of essays *So Here We Are* will appear from Shearsman Books in early 2011. He edits international literary magazine Tears in the Fence and regularly reviews for The Use Of English and other journals. He is the Script Editor and a scriptwriter for Middle Ditch, the internet drama serial at middleditch.blogspot.com.

# ARRANGING EXCURSIONS
# TO DISPARATE WORLDS

Simon Turner anticipates an Oulipian invasion of
contemporary British poetry

1991 – when Nirvana topped the charts with their second album, *Nevermind*,
opening the floodgates for a series of kindred, though lesser, bands
(Soundgarden, Smashing Pumpkins, Pearl Jam and a whole host of other
groups your mother wouldn't approve of) to assault the barricades of
popular culture – is known in certain circles as 'the year punk broke'. In a
similar vein, I believe that future literary historians will refer to 2009 as 'the
year that the avant-garde finally made a dent in the public imagination.'

The evidence, though wildly subjective in its implications, consists
of three exhibits. Here, for what they're worth, are the facts as they stand:

*Exhibit A*

In the run-up to Christmas 2008, something rather odd happened in the
world of broadsheet book reviewing. A collection of formally experimental
prose poems written in a distinctly avant-garde mode by a little-known
Canadian poet – which, in the context of a literary culture that routinely
ignores Canadian literature unless it's been churned from the Atwood
millwheels, is an achievement in itself – began to receive a great deal of press
attention, with coverage in the *Telegraph*, the *Guardian*, and Radio 4's *Today*
programme, finding its way, with astonishing speed, onto the bestseller

lists.[1]

*Exhibit B*

A formally experimental novel, composed entirely in photographs and captions, by an obscure American artist and designer, best-known for producing the titles for Noah Baumbach's mumblecore classic *The Squid and the Whale*, was the subject of a Hollywood bidding war involving such luminaries as Brad Pitt and Julia Roberts. The movie is currently in pre-production, with Pitt and Nathalie Portman touted as the leads.[2] To the best of my knowledge this has never happened to a Stewart Home novel.

*Exhibit C*

In November 2009, Radio 4 broadcast a programme on a little-known, formally experimental French literary movement – there's a pattern emerging – hosted by Britain's favourite compilationist[3] and best-selling author, Ben Schott.

For the uninformed, the surprise Canadian Christmas hit was *Eunoia* by Christian Bök; Leanne Shapton's *Artifacts* (or to give its full title, *Important Artifacts and Personal Property from the Collection of Lenore Doolan and Harold Morris: Including Books, Street Fashion and Jewelry*) was the genre-hopping conceptual oddity that Brad Pitt so badly wanted to star in; the obscure clique of (mostly) French avant-gardists highlighted by Ben Schott for the Big British Castle was, of course, the Oulipo; and what the disparate phenomena catalogued above collectively represent, I would argue, is the visible peak of a quiet but potentially revolutionary turn in British literature. The Oulipians have very much arrived, and their presence on the scene could well prove to have a profound effect upon our long-held conceptions of literary form, potentially and irrevocably altering the course of contemporary British poetry.

These are, I am aware, bold claims, and I hope to justify them in due course; but before I get to the meat of my argument, a little history is probably required. The Oulipo, or the *Ouvroir de littérature potentielle* (which translates as the 'workshop for potential literature'), came into being in the early 1960s. Founded by Raymond Queneau and Francois Le Lionnais,[4] the group sought to expand the parameters of literature through the application of severe constraints, often, though not exclusively, derived from mathematical procedures (many leading Oulipians have been mathematicians and scientists). The Oulipo has numbered amongst its ranks some of the most prestigious names of 20th century literature, including Georges Perec, Raymond Queneau, and Italo Calvino, whilst the group's activities have attracted the attention of equally notable literary figures, including John Ashbery and Paul Auster.

In many regards, the Oulipo are an awkward and egregious bunch, even by the standards of the post-war avant-garde (a species not generally known for its loose-limbed party-hopping bonhomie). This is due in no small part to the fact that Oulipians, with their perverse tendency to invent new forms which are almost baroque in their severity and complexity, stand Canute-like in isolate opposition to the tidal currents of 20th century poetics. Indeed, for those of us who prefer our literary criticism to come fully equipped with a teleological narrative arc, the drift of 20th century literature in general (and poetry in particular) has suggested a movement away from traditional conceptions of form towards the brave new world of *vers libre* and its numerous unruly children. Modernism and the various other *isms* which erupted around it – Surrealism, Vorticism, Futurism, Constructivism, Objectivism – all asserted, to a greater or lesser extent, the freedom of language and its relation to personal expression. Form, for the avant-garde, could be said to come into being in the process of composition: it is manifestly *not* a pre-existing set of rules and procedures that one might follow to the letter, like the instructions for an Airfix model. Rather, form, as Charles Olson asserts, quoting Robert Creeley in his landmark essay of 1950, 'Projective Verse', 'IS NEVER MORE THAN AN EXTENSION OF CONTENT.'[5]

Consequently, *form* in its classical sense becomes almost impossible to discuss in relation to high Modernism and its post-avant children, whilst *style* is elevated to the status of a secular religion: just consider the number of adjectival modifiers – Jamesian, Joycean, Eliotean, Lawrentian, Steinian, Poundian, Conradian – which the founding mothers and fathers of Modernism bequeathed to the world. Which is not to say that the *Cantos* or *The Waste Land* are formless to any extent that matters, simply that their forms cannot be reduced to a series of rules for the curious student to follow, in the manner of the sonnet or the villanelle: their form, rather, is entirely bound up with the process of composition, so that the poem cannot be distinguished, ultimately, from the personality of its author, just as Olson's *Maximus* poems, for all they owe to Pound, are Olson's and Olson's alone, and Chris Torrance's *Magic Door*, whilst 'Olsonian' in composition, equally represents Torrance's own unique use of the same open form.

None of this would be of any import at all were there not a coded value judgement written into the avant-garde's conception of form. That is to say, to conceive of form as something that the poem or the novel must be liberated *from* is to read literary freedom in decidedly political or revolutionary terms. The result, in both the UK and the States, at least in the post-war period, has been a bipartisan literary environment where the various experimental or post-avant cliques have, for a great deal of the time, read any adherence to form as a regression into a reactionary mindset. The mainstream, in its turn, has proven itself to be decidedly unfriendly to experimental poetics. A little of the flavour of this literary deadlock can be gleaned from the following passage, taken from Ron Silliman's idiosyncratic memoir of 2004, *Under Albany*:

> Form proposes its telos: "I know just how many lines this sonnet will take." In 1981, when I wrote "Albany", there was still significant controversy over the deliberately "inorganic" elements of my poetry, especially the use of repetition in *Ketjak* and the Fibonacci number system in *Tjanting* [...]

As Silliman goes on to ask of himself and his readers, 'Was I "betraying" my literary ancestors [...]?'[6] This seems like startlingly emotive language ('Controversy'? 'Betrayal'? Really?) to use in relation to a relatively innocuous point of aesthetic discussion, but read in the context of the bitter rivalries between mainstream and post-avant poetics that continue to dominate the literary landscape, Silliman's self-questioning in this passage makes perfect sense. Of course, writing in form *is* a kind of 'betrayal', an act of apostasy in rebellion against the post-modernist dictates of Olson and his descendents.

In Britain, the 'binary myths', to borrow Andy Brown's evocative phrase, of contemporary poetry reached their nadir, and apotheosis, during the so-called 'Poetry Wars' of the 1970s, when a number of left-field poets affiliated with the British Poetry Revival were elected to the leadership of the Poetry Society, much to the chagrin of the (aesthetically) conservative old guard.[7] In many ways, contemporary poetry in the UK still bears the scars of that period, with broadsides being fired from both camps at regular intervals: witness, for example, Niall McDevitt's forceful and entertaining polemic, 'Contra Avant Garde', in issue 13 of *The Wolf*,[8] or Don Paterson's pomo-baiting introduction to *New British Poetry*,[9] if you want to gain a sense of the mainstream position on the matter. From the experimental camp, meanwhile, we might look to Jeffrey Side's critique of Seamus Heaney,[10] and Gabriel Josipovici's recent vigorous and biting defence of modernism against the banalities of Ian McEwan and his BritFic cohorts,[11] for evidence of an equally indecorous counter-argument. Reading these manifestos and intellectual sorties, one feels as though there is an absence of middle ground, a failure of language taking place: form, it would seem, means something altogether different to both camps, and much of the animosity arises from this central, ineradicable fact.

The Oulipo, then, offers the possibility of something approaching a rapprochement between the opposing forces. Or, if not a rapprochement precisely, then Oulipian procedures and restraints, at the very least, offer a new language of form that the mainstream and experimental cliques can agree upon. Their emphasis on the process of composition allows the avant-garde to embrace them, as they still adhere in many regards to the Olsonian equation of form and content cited above. Yet, more importantly, they have collectively contributed a number of devices and procedures – including the lipogram, homophonic translation, and the N+7 technique[12] – that are entirely continuous with the acceptable restraints of classical formalism, such as the sonnet, the sestina, and the villanelle. The transparency of Oulipian procedures is part of their appeal: their appearance as part of a number of creative writing degree courses, including those of Warwick, Exeter and Birmingham, is testament to this fact. Indeed, Philip Terry, himself a prolific Oulipian, teaches a course on constrained writing at the University of Essex.

A number of recent anthologies of British poetry have made a point of emphasising their commitment to formal and stylistic diversity, in ways which mirror the 'third way' poetics of the path-finding American anthology *American Hybrid* (2009)[13]. This is certainly commendable, but the editors of these anthologies are frustratingly vague as to what 'formal diversity' might consist of. Claire Pollard and James Byrne, the editors of *Voice Recognition: 21 Poets for the 21st Century* (2009), assert that they 'sought a healthy approach to diversity' in making their editorial decisions, arguing that 'there are meaningful explorations of relationships between page and performance, modernist and post-modern, experimental and avant garde' in their selection.[14] A noble sentiment, certainly, but the editors make no real attempt to narrow and define their terms. Tom Chivers, in his introduction to *City State: New London Poetry* (2009), is comparably broad in his use of terminology: 'The poets in *City State*,' he writes, 'range in age from late teens to mid-thirties, in aesthetic from formalist to performance to post-avant and back again.'[15] Again, the sentiment is agreeable, as is the anthology itself, but the sheer broadness of terms such as 'formalist' and 'post-avant' is deeply problematic, and undermines Chivers' otherwise exemplary editorial decisions.

In his introduction to *Identity Parade: New British & Irish Poets* (2010), Roddy Lumsden is perhaps the most successful of the recent anthologists in his explication of his editorial processes, and he takes great care in grounding his anthology's commitment to diversity in terms both historical and aesthetic. However, I would take issue with the 'essential individualism' that Lumsden detects in the poets he has surveyed and collated, and am particularly troubled by his assertion that 'this might well be the generation of poets least driven by movements, fashions, conceptual and stylistic sharing.' Of course, I realise I am only taking the bait that Lumsden has knowingly planted – he suggests as much when he asserts that 'critics and academics will seek – and find – traits and trends in the larger bodies of work represented here'[16] – but nonetheless I cannot resist taking up the challenge. My own belief is that trends *are* detectable, that stylistic sharing *is* taking place, and that if formal and stylistic diversity are to become the norm in British poetics, as the editors cited suggest, we would do worse than look to the Oulipo for guidance. Indeed, a significant number of writers are already doing so, and are producing a vibrant and original body of work as a result.

The poets I have chosen to discuss – Jeremy Over, Matthew Welton and James Wilkes – are not only formally and aesthetically distinct from one another, but their individual oeuvres are also highly various and multivocal in character. Their linguistic inventiveness – one might even be tempted to say adventurousness – is a direct result of their adherence to Oulipo-derived praxis. Moreover, all three authors are in the early stages of their literary careers, which means that their investigation of Oulipian procedures is not a late-blooming and short-lived infatuation with the continental avant-garde, but is central to their identities as poets. What unites these poets, however, is a sense of fun, of the almost infinite possibilities inherent in the language which are unleashed through the application of restraints and formal procedures. Whatever one thinks of the Oulipo, the introduction of their procedures and concerns to contemporary British poetry can only have an enlivening effect.

Of the three poets, Wilkes is the least visibly and classically 'Oulipian' in his concerns. His debut collection, *Weather A System* (2009), is marked by the same formal variety and ingenuity detectable in Welton and Over, but a cursory examination does not suggest that this is specifically

Oulipian in intent. Indeed, Iain Sinclair is the most overt influence on the collection, particularly apparent in the psychogeographical 'Purbeck Poems' that form the heart of *Weather A System*, and seems to be a far more abiding *genius loci* for Wilkes' imagination than, say, Perec or Jacques Roubaud. However, closer attention yields a very different picture. For example, what is 'Medical Questionnaire', the poem with which *Weather A System* opens, if not a piece written according to the formal constraints suggested by its title? Who but a thorough-going child of the Oulipo would include a homophonic translation of César Vallejo ('Remedy all cooks to roué. Eeeeee! Hisss!'),[17] or write a series of 'Four Variations on the Same Midwinter'?

However, it is in his mastery of a particular form – the 'brazzle' – that Wilkes shows his true Oulipian credentials. The brazzle is, according to the *Oulipo Compendium*, a kind of fake book review or blurb, the title of whose subject is arrived at through a process of phonetic extrapolation applied to an existing title and author (*Ulysses*, for example, yields *The Christmas Snake Murder*, via 'yule – hiss – ease' and a subsequent series of sonic and semantic mutations).[18] I have no idea how Wilkes arrived at his various titles – *Delta Blueprints* by Pieter Peeters, Gareth Jenkins' *Handles Brusquely* and *The Leaping Pebble* by Robert Steinbeck[19] are three of my personal favourites – but the brilliance of these poems lies not in the hidden process of their construction, but rather in the wicked fun resulting from Wilkes' free play within the strictures of the review form. His 'review' of Steinbeck's novel, for example, opens with the reviewer-speak shorthand of '*x* meets *y*', but in Wilkes' hands, this lazy formulation becomes something strange and comic: 'Speculative biomedical ethics meets dancehall reverie in this elegant folio reprint of the hard-to-find private press original (1908)' (32). Like Borges, Wilkes creates entire worlds from footnotes and literary ephemera: in the mangled logic of these reviews, it seems perfectly reasonable that Steinbeck's book should be the basis for a movie starring Robert Redford, in which the protagonist 'attempt[s] to fence DNA stolen from a medieval saint's fingerbone' (32), or that John Seesman, the author of *Caliphate Pop* (a book I would kill to have on my bookshelf) should have produced another volume entitled *Celtic Horse Mysteries for Your Cat* (37). Indeed, if *Weather A System* can be said to have a unifying intent, it is the creation of

**Wilkes creates mystery and poetry from the ephemeral**

mystery and poetry from the ephemeral, the broken, the discarded. Tellingly, the collection concludes with a series of 'Fountain Transcripts', which, the author informs us, 'faithfully reconstitute conversations between Lawrence Bradby, Sally Davies, Lina Hakim and James Wilkes that took place as they drifted around London looking for fountains one Saturday in 2009' (59). A total adherence to recorded fact – if, indeed, we can take Wilkes' assertion at face value[20] – might be construed as the ultimate literary constraint.

Matthew Welton's second collection, *We needed coffee but...*[21] is, like Wilkes' debut, concerned with the ephemera of the everyday, but Welton differs in his conception of form. There is an architectural quality to the poems in *We needed coffee but...*, a sense of scale and near-infinite linguistic possibility. Welton's forte is a brand of permutational Oulipianism, whereby a number of imagistic and semantic elements are recycled and recombined in musically-minded variations, producing new effects each time. The most ambitious piece in the collection, 'South Korea and Japan 2002', operates according to the processes of football fixtures: each element in the text is analogous to a team in 2002's World Cup, and as each 'match' is played, a new combination is created. And, as with the World Cup, the combinations narrow as certain teams in the fixtures are eliminated, and others go through. All this formal ingenuity would be meaningless, however, were the writing of no interest in itself, but Welton is, thankfully, a formidable and elegant phrasemaker. '07 June   Sapporo Dome, Japan', for example, one of the 'games' in the 'Group Stage' sequence, proffers the following beguiling image: 'There's a kind of argy-bargy in the rainclouds and the sun, and the colour of the light in the low summer sky engorges through the trees and flowers' (59). What is notable here, to my mind, is the way in which Welton handles quotidian language unobtrusively, yet effectively: there is nothing showy or 'poetic' about his vocabulary – 'argy-bargy', in particular, is wonderfully earthy, and entirely in keeping with a sequence that borrows its formal restraints from the beautiful game – but the passage nonetheless has a rhythmic fluidity and musical cadence of its own.

Welton's interest in permutational literature deliberately draws attention to the essentially constructed nature of syntax, suggesting that language – even manifested in its most basic components – is a trap, and the concept of free expression a hubristic illusion. In some pieces – the overly repetitious 'Dr Suss', for example – Welton's compositional concerns with syntax and structure lead him down some blind (and, for the reader, maddening) alleys: the work of art becomes reduced to a philosophical endurance test, closely akin to the minimalist compositions of Terry Riley or Steve Reich. Welton is at his best, and most acute, when his experiments in form are brief enough not to outstay their welcome. 'I must say that at first it was difficult work', a tribute to the fiendishly complex compositional method of Raymond Roussel,[22] one of the Oulipo's 'anticipatory plagiarist' forefathers, is far more effective an expression of Welton's concerns as a writer than 'Dr Suss', built as it is around sonic rather than semantic repetition:

Aramaic inverts the intransitive verbs
As potatoes emerge from the depths of the earth
I'm arranging excursions to disparate worlds
I'm assured there's a version that's technically worse (52)

'Four-letter words', meanwhile, which arguably employs Welton's trickiest procedure – the poem is composed entirely in (you guessed it) words of four letters – draws attention to the essential fallacy of the avant-garde dream of form as an organic outgrowth of content. Here, Welton's restrictive formal decision determines entirely what can and cannot be spoken – in other words, content follows form – as the poem drives itself forward with a string of aggressively declarative sentences: 'Push your door shut. Turn down your lamp. | Pour your self some coke. Grab some blue-bean soup' (35). What the world needs now is a novel of Dickensian proportions written in the very same form.

If Welton provides a welcome antidote to the myth of avant-garde impenetrability – how difficult, precisely, can a writer be who has an endorsement from Dave Gorman on the cover of his book? – Jeremy Over, arguably the most classically Oulipian of my triumvirate, exemplifies to an even greater extent the ludic possibilities inherent in the literature of constraint. Over's second collection, *Deceiving Wild Creatures* (2009), is without doubt messier, more anarchic than either *Weather A System* or *We needed coffee but...*, yet

# Welton provides a welcome antidote to the myth of avant-garde impenetrability

it is also in many respects more approachable. I am loathe to label Over a comic poet, in case it raises the spectre of Pam Ayres, but much of *Deceiving Wild Creatures* is extremely funny. 'Killer in the Rain', a pantoum built out of phrases lifted from Raymond Chandler (extremely Oulipian in that it employs not one but two restrictions in its composition) is typical of Over's humour. Divorced from their context, and rendered nonsensical through the repetition demanded by the pantoum form, Chandler's hardboiled style comes across as comically deranged:

> Nothing more happened.
> I had another hunch.
> I poked it under her nose,
> then I ran away.

> I had another hunch
> that stopped the door closing,
> then I ran away.
> I don't know why [...][23]

In many ways, Over is simply having fun here, but his choice of Raymond Chandler (the granddaddy of American crime fiction) as a source text is both canny and instructive, suggesting the degree to which narrative and generic conventions are always already one step away from self-parody.

Recontextualisation, in fact, forms the basis for many of the poems in the collection, and like Wilkes and Welton, Over seems animated by a poetics of the ephemeral. 'Whip Tim Kelly', for example, is composed of various colloquial attempts to render birdsong as recognisable human speech ('Quick, three beers | More pork, more pork | A little bit of bread and no cheese' (27)), whilst 'The North Cumbrian Coast' plucks phrases and passages from a historical guidebook to the area to construct a fractured narrative of absence and loss: a place-name or location is scarcely mentioned before its annihilation is assured by historical circumstance, either as a result of an act of violence ('NEW MAWBRAY was pillaged by the Scots in 1216 and 1322' (68)), or through assaults originating in the natural world (as in the case of ROCKCLIFFE, whose '1,000 sheep were drowned on the marshes when there was a 24ft tide and gale' (67)). In another instance, Over uncovers the unintentional poetry of autistic children, as he compiles found phrases from '*Hans Asperger's paper on autism in childhood*': the results ('Well the lake it can never be as long and never have that many branches not in the least little bit' (33)) will no doubt look familiar to fans of Gertrude Stein's *Tender Buttons*.

Over's attention to the ephemeral and discarded is, in addition, of significance to the more conventional pieces in *Deceiving Wild Creatures*. In 'Birthday Haibun' – although not Oulipian *per se*, it is telling that this poem, in memory of Roger Deakin, should be written in a long-established Japanese form – the narrator's close attention to small details leads to the quiet revelation that wagtails are misnamed: 'I wonder,' writes Over, 'why they wag their tails and then notice that it isn't. It's *tapping* it up and down. I've known smokers tap their cigarettes like that, constantly, so that the ash doesn't get a chance to accumulate' (64). Such structural variety, in fact, lends *Deceiving Wild Creatures* the character of an anthology, a compendium of strange and remarkable forms, which the reader is welcome, in true *Blue Peter* fashion, to make at home. (This impression is compounded by the presence of two ironic 'how to' poems – 'Poetry should be made by all' – which suggest an attempt, though comic in intent, to democratise, and render approachable, avant-garde compositional practices.) Over's wide-ranging magpie method of composition, in fact, coupled to his refusal to treat the giants of literary modernism with undue seriousness, combine to make *Deceiving Wild Creatures* an exemplary Oulipian work, and something of a yardstick by which formally experimental work might be measured in the future.

Harry Mathews, the Oulipo's most prolific and notable American practitioner, has argued: 'From the reader's point of view, the existence in literature of potentiality in its Oulipian sense has the charm of introducing duplicity into all written texts, whether Oulipian or not,' going on to assert: 'The fine surface unity that a piece of writing proposes is belied and beleaguered; behind it, in the realm of potentiality, a dialectic has emerged.'[24] In this sense, at any rate, my essay can be read as a distinctly Oulipian text, in that its 'belied and beleaguered' surface is haunted at every turn by the various aborted drafts which preceded it. In a variety of alternative worlds, this essay has no doubt taken the form, as it often promised to in the process of writing, of a utopian screed, or a literary memoir, or a raging manifesto in defence of extreme formalism.

Whatever form it might have taken, however, this essay was never intended to be anything other than provisional and subjective. The three authors I have surveyed, exemplary Oulipians all, are illustrative of a literary trend which is far broader, far more diffuse, than I have been able to suggest in the space allotted. I might easily have tackled, had there been time, John Goodby's *Uncaged Sea* (2008), an acrostic 'read-through' of Dylan Thomas' *Collected Poems*; Andy Brown's recent excursions into the world of Oulipian riddles; Philip Terry's two volumes of *Oulipoems*; or David Morley's wonderfully eclectic approach to form in *Scientific Papers* (2002) and *The Invisible Kings* (2007). My essay, too, has somewhat elided the small but notable body of Oulipian fiction to have emerged in recent years, including Richard Beard's *X20* (1996) and *Damascus* (1998); Dan Rhodes' *Anthropology* (2000), a collection of 101 short stories, each containing only 101 words; and Paul Griffiths' *let me tell you* (2008), composed using only those words spoken by Ophelia in *Hamlet*. Beyond the confines of the printed word, *Found in Translation*, a serio-comic lecture written and performed by Joe Dunthorne, Ross Sutherland and Tim Clare, detailing the writers' various failed attempts to gain entry into the Oulipo, has stealthily smuggled the aesthetics of extreme formalism into the slam and stand-up poetry circuits.

My essay has, of course, been provisional in another, more important sense as well. Wilkes, Over and Welton are only, I believe, the first wave of an Oulipian invasion of British literature; an invasion which will undoubtedly have a positive effect on British poetry. If nothing else, Oulipian techniques might provide, at last, a shared language of form within which the mainstream and experimental camps can continue to wage their wars of attrition. They may not agree on anything else – indeed, it would be a tedious literary environment if we all agreed on every topic – but a common aesthetic language is, at the very least, a starting point. In so many ways, the potential of potential literature in relation to British poetry has only just begun to be realised.

## Notes

[1] According to a *Times* article on the subject, the book's entire British print run sold out in a matter of hours after the *Today* appearance. Giles Whittell, 'Eunoia: the Good Bök', the *Times*, November 14th 2008, accessed at http://entertainment.timesonline.co.uk/tol/arts_and_entertainment/books/article5153956.ece on August 3rd 2010.

[2] Janine di Giovanni, 'Artifacts by Leanne Shapton', in the *Times*, November 7 2009, accessed at http://entertainment.timesonline.co.uk/tol/arts_and_entertainment/books/fiction/article6904929.ece on August 3rd 2010.

[3] Is that a word? It is now.

[4] Alastair Brotchie, 'Introduction', in Raymond Queneau et al, *Oulipo Laboratory* (London: Atlas Press, 1995), ix.

[5] Charles Olson, *Collected Prose*, eds., Donald Allen and Benjamin Friedlander (Berkeley, CA: University of California Press, 1997), 240.

[6] Ron Silliman, *Under Albany* (Cambridge: Salt, 2004), 20-21.

[7] See Peter Barry's *Poetry Wars: British Poetry of the 1970s and the Battle of Earls Court* (Cambridge: Salt, 2006) for a full account of the period.

[8] Niall McDevitt, 'Contra Avant Garde', in *The Wolf* Issue 13, Autumn 2006, 40-44.

[9] Don Paterson and Charles Simic, eds., *New British Poetry* (Minneapolis, MN: Graywolf Press, 2004).

[10] Side's article, and the responses it has provoked, are archived at *Jacket Magazine*'s homepage: http://jacketmagazine.com/00/home.shtml.

[11] Gabriel Josipovici, *What Ever Happened to Modernism?* (London and New Haven, CT: Yale University Press, 2010).

[12] The lipogram is a mode of composition in which certain letters are excluded. The most famous lipogram, *La Disparition* by Georges Perec, was composed without once using the letter e. Homophonic translation, meanwhile, is a mode of translating texts that favours sound over sense. In the case of N+7, new texts are generated by taking an existing piece of writing, and replacing its nouns with their equivalents found seven places along in the dictionary.

[13] Cole Swensen and David St. John, eds., *American Hybrid* (New York, NY: W. W. Norton and Co., 2009).

[14] James Byrne and Clare Pollard, eds., *Voice Recognition: 21 Poets for the 21st Century* (Newcastle: Bloodaxe, 2009), 13.

[15] Tom Chivers, ed., *City State: New London Poetry* (London: Penned in the Margins, 2009), 9.

[16] Roddy Lumsden, ed., *Identity Parade: New British & Irish Poets* (Newcastle: Bloodaxe, 2010), 19.

[17] James Wilkes, *Weather A System* (London: Penned in the Margins, 2009), 62. Subsequent references will appear parenthetically in the main body of the essay.

[18] Harry Mathews and Alastair Brotchie, eds., *Oulipo Compendium* (London: Atlas Press, 2005), 95.

[19] It is not stated whether this Steinbeck is any relation to the author of *The Grapes of Wrath*, but an affinity can, I believe, be reasonably assumed.

[20] There is precedent for the use of recorded material in literature: large portions of Jack Kerouac's novel *Visions of Cody* take the form of transcripts of conversations between Kerouac and Neal Cassady, though the novel contains its own negation, in that the

transcripts are immediately followed by Kerouac's attempt to imitate them. Given that Wilkes' own transcripts are printed in a context that also includes reviews of books that never existed and the non-semantic translation of foreign-language texts, there is no reason to believe that the transcripts are any more grounded in fact. Their possible duplicity could, of course, be at least partly the point of the exercise.

[21] Its full title, a poem in itself, reads: 'We needed coffee but we'd got ourselves convinced that the later we left it the better it would taste, and, as the country grew flatter and the roads became quiet and dusk began to colour the sky, you could guess from the way we retuned the radio and unfolded the map or commented on the view that the tang of determination had overtaken our thoughts, and, when, fidgety and untalkative but almost home, we drew up outside the all-night restaurant, it felt like we might just stay in the car, listening to the engine and the gentle wind.' Matthew Welton, *We needed coffee but...* (Manchester: Carcanet, 2009), 3. Subsequent references will appear parenthetically in the main body of the essay.

[22] Outlined in Roussel's teasing, and possibly entirely fictional, essay, 'How I Wrote Certain of My Books', in Roussel, *How I Wrote Certain of My Books*, Trevor Winkfield, ed. (Boston, MA: Exact Change, 1995), 3-28.

[23] Jeremy Over, *Deceiving Wild Creatures* (Manchester: Carcanet, 2009), 23. Subsequent references will appear parenthetically in the main body of the essay.

[24] Harry Mathews, *The Case of the Persevering Maltese: Collected Essays* (Champaign, IL, and London: Dalkey Archive Press, 2003), 301.

## Further reading

Peter Barry, *Poetry Wars: British Poetry of the 1970s and the Battle of Earls Court* (Cambridge: Salt, 2006).

Richard Beard, *Damascus* (London: Flamingo, 1998).

\_\_\_\_, *X20* (London: Vintage, 2005).

Christian Bök, *Eunoia* (London: Canongate, 2009).

James Byrne and Clare Pollard (eds.), *Voice Recognition: 21 Poets for the 21ˢᵗ Century* (Newcastle: Bloodaxe, 2009).

Tom Chivers (ed.), *City State: New London Poetry* (London: Penned in the Margins, 2009).

John Goodby, *Uncaged Sea* (Hove: Waterloo Press, 2008).

Paul Griffiths, *let me tell you* (Hastings: Reality Street, 2008).

Gabriel Josipovici, *What Ever Happened to Modernism?* (London and New Haven, CT: Yale University Press, 2010).

Jack Kerouac, *Visions of Cody* (London: Flamingo, 1995).

Roddy Lumsden, (ed.), *Identity Parade: New British & Irish Poets* (Newcastle: Bloodaxe, 2010).

Harry Mathews and Alastair Brotchie (eds.), *Oulipo Compendium* (London: Atlas Press, 2005).

Harry Mathews, *The Case of the Persevering Maltese: Collected Essays* (Champaign, IL: Dalkey Archive Press, 2003).

Niall McDevitt, 'Contra Avant Garde', in *The Wolf*, Issue 13, Autumn 2006, 40-44.

David Morley, *Scientific Papers* (Manchester: Carcanet, 2002).

_____, *The Invisible Kings* (Manchester: Carcanet, 2007).

Charles Olson, *Collected Prose*, ed. Donald Allen and Benjamin Friedlander (Berkeley, CA: University of California Press, 1997).

Jeremy Over, *Deceiving Wild Creatures* (Manchester: Carcanet, 2009).

Raymond Queneau, et al, *Oulipo Laboratory* (London: Atlas Press, 1995).

Dan Rhodes, *Anthropology* (London: Fourth Estate, 2001).

Raymond Roussel, *How I Wrote Certain of My Books*, ed. Trevor Winkfield (Boston, MA: Exact Change, 1995).

Leanne Shapton, *Important Artifacts and Personal Property from the Collection of Lenore Doolan and Harold Morris, Including Books, Street Fashion and Jewelry* (London: Bloomsbury, 2009).

Ron Silliman, *Under Albany* (Cambridge: Salt, 2004).

Cole Swensen and David St. John (eds.), *American Hybrid* (New York, NY: W. W. Norton and Co., 2009).

Philip Terry, *Oulipoems* (Tokyo and Toronto: Ahadada Books, 2007).

____, *Oulipoems 2* (Tokyo and Toronto: Ahadada Books, 2009).

Matthew Welton, *We needed coffee, but...* (Manchester: Carcanet, 2009).

James Wilkes, *Weather A System* (London: Penned in the Margins, 2009).

Simon Turner was born in Birmingham in 1980. His poems and reviews have appeared in a number of publications, including Tears in the Fence, Horizon Review, Poetry Salzburg and The Wolf. His first collection, *You Are Here*, was published by Heaventree in 2007. His second, *Difficult Second Album*, appeared from Nine Arches Press in 2010. With George Ttoouli, he co-edits the blogzine Gists and Piths. Forthcoming projects include an edited collection of essays on British Surrealism and a critical study of civilian war poetry. He lives and works in Warwickshire.

# SLAM: A POETIC DIALOGUE

Tim Clare makes the case for and against the competitive
live poetry phenomenon

Plato wanted poets disbarred from his republic. He lumped them together
with the Sophists, crass populist conjurors who used the power of rhetoric
to deceive and beguile, rather than committing themselves to the search for
'truth'.

Plato never put scare quotes around truth, obviously. That's a
flourish added by me, every inch a product of this fallen, fractal, postmodern
world we find ourselves in. The point is, if you think about it, Plato's take
on poets is really rather flattering. Underhanded demagoguery or no, he's
saying that poets have power. That poetry can, you know, influence people;
to a dangerous degree, in fact.

I like to think of Slam Poetry as the living embodiment of
Plato's worst fears. Practitioners and advocates often hold it up as the
democratisation of the artform. To many outside of the scene, Slam Poetry's
particular flavour of democratisation – performers competing live against
one another for audience approval; random judges ascribing aesthetic worth
via a numerical score – is precisely what kills poetry as art.

The resulting bun fight has been played out many times over the
past few decades, but I shall attempt to summarise both sides' arguments –
as I understand them – in their strongest possible forms:

Slamophiles contend that their critics are the self-appointed gatekeepers of a crumbling poetry elite, rattled at the realisation that direct engagement with audiences makes them redundant. Slam exists outside the echo chamber of academia; its consumers aren't expected to recognise abstruse Classical references or reductive, self-indulgent conversations with previous writers. Slam Poetry can be understood by the archetypal man or woman on the

## Slam exists outside the echo chamber of academia

street, but more than that, it values the opinion of the casual listener just as much as the judgement of a supposed expert steeped in the tropes and traditions of the form. It is precisely this 'one person, one vote' principle of democracy that terrifies poetry's old guard the most, because it allows for no privileged voices, no bellwethers to steer the flock. Slam's loudest detractors, therefore, are those who believe they enjoy a certain amount of status as cultural commentators and wish to maintain the status quo. Moreover, unlike practitioners of traditional and page forms, Slam poets do not enjoy the luxury of shielding their work from criticism behind a bulwark of recondite theory and glib relativism. Although there is plenty of room for nuance in an audience's response, in the end, analysing a Slam poem's reception is refreshingly binary: either it wins, or it doesn't.

Finally – and in the white heat of argument, the pro-Slam lobby often forget this – it's not meant to be taken too seriously. Slam founding father Marc Smith's 1984 proto-slam took place inside a boxing ring and was essentially a piece of comic performance art. Integral to Slam's original ethos was to strip away the layers of pretention and create a live spectacle that – whatever else it manages to achieve along the way – exists first and foremost as entertainment.

At this juncture in the dialogue we can imagine our 'traditional' or 'page' poet – who bristles at this sloppy use of terminology but for now, lets it lie, keen not to wage war on two fronts – taking a sip of water, then cracking his or her knuckles as he or she sets about responding with gusto.

Firstly, let's deal with this claim of 'democratisation', the notion that, in the words of Marc Smith, 'slam gives [poetry] back to the people'. Does it? Who are these hypothetical 'people' you refer to? Since when did poetry lovers cease to qualify as 'people'? When did being conversant with and passionate about your craft become grounds for shame? Slam doesn't give poetry back to the people, it just thumbs its nose at one perceived elite by ringfencing the form on behalf of another.

If you were truly democratising poetry then everyone present would read and perform, listen to everyone else, and offer feedback. Hello? We already have that over here in the 'poetry establishment' – it's called a writing group, or a workshop, or an open mic night. The difference is, at those, the pieces you write aren't restricted to being under three minutes, and we don't penalise poets who don't memorise their work, or who prefer not to act out every line like a dramatic monologue. In fact, some poets prefer not to read their work out at all – maybe because they're shy, maybe because they just think it works better on the page – and we have online forums and magazines where they can share their work too. Where do they fit into your 'democratisation' of poetry? Do they qualify as 'people'?

Your folksy claim that Slam is aimed at the common man and woman doesn't pass the smell test either. Almost all of your events have a door charge, and they're advertised as Slam Poetry, so your crowd is self-selecting. Slam has regulars, an in-crowd, and an elite in exactly the same way that all other forms of poetry do. There is no evidence that a Slam Poetry crowd is any more diverse than the audience for page poetry. Indeed, the emergence of recurring themes and stratagems in popular Slam poems suggests that the form attracts a very specific type of demographic.

In fact, let's not beat around the bush – Slam, heterogeneity is not your strong suit. Typically, a successful Slam poem will take one of two forms:

i) a first-person identity politics monologue championing the position of an ostensibly marginalised voice;

ii) the presentation of a strawman argument – typically conservative – which the poet proceeds to tear apart, often humorously.

Particularly accomplished Slammers may combine the two in one poem. It would be nice to think of this as satirical oversimplification but it is not. At the time of writing, the most watched Slam Poetry video on Youtube is Taylor Mali's 'What Teachers Make', a piece in which he heroically takes to task an (imaginary) obnoxious lawyer at a dinner party. The lawyer is presented as a haughty, avaricious grotesque, sneeringly dismissing the entire teaching profession, before conveniently providing a setup that allows the poet to spend the next two and a half minutes yelling about what a fantastic human being he is. The crowd applaud and whoop, even though this dialogue never actually took place, and even though Mali never argues for teachers as a whole, but merely his own professional brilliance.

Slam Poetry isn't really about poetry at all. Everything you need to know about Slam you can learn from Schopenhauer's *The Art Of Controversy* – a compendium of dirty rhetorical tricks one can use to wrong-foot one's opponent in a public debate. The book reads as a startlingly prescient 'How To Slam' handbook, with chapter titles such as 'Generalise Your Opponent's Specific Statements', 'Choose Metaphors Favourable To Your Proposition', 'Persuade The Audience, Not The Opponent', 'Bewilder Your Opponent By Mere Bombast' and finally 'Become Personal, Insulting, Rude': all standard rhetorical plays in the Slam world. Yes, you occasionally encounter a self-deprecating piece, or a comic anecdote, but these will always lose against impassioned stump speeches ostensibly on behalf of the oppressed.

Here, our Slam poet can no longer restrain him or herself, and butts in, because come on, now you're doing exactly what you accuse us of doing – generalising from a single instance, presenting a strawman caricature of the form then attacking that rather than the form itself, and resorting to insults. Yes, it's true that Slam has influences other than poetry – that's part of its richness. America, the birthplace of Slam, has a proud tradition of passionate, persuasive public speaking, from Charismatic preachers to the leaders of the Civil Rights movement. And before you dismiss Slam as ideologically homogenous, you need to recognise that it exists as part of a wider cultural dialectic, responding to messages pushed by corporate interests in advertising, for instance, or violent, homophobic lyrics in hip-hop. Slam nights provide a supportive atmosphere where the disenfranchised can feel safe getting on stage and answering back to groups who would deny them freedoms. If that means that a few white, middle-class men have to work a bit harder to make it through to the final, well – I'm sure they'll cope somehow.

But, retorts our traditional poet, by institutionalising that narrative and turning it into a competitive sport, Slam has cheapened it. Poets have a clear inducement to fake personal disclosure, and a strong disincentive to present anything that might challenge, or run contrary to the crowd's established views. Providing a

## Slam poets have a clear inducement to fake personal disclosure

supportive atmosphere for marginalised voices is all well and good, but don't pretend it constitutes freedom of speech. Slam Poetry is every bit as much an echo chamber as you claim traditional poetry is.

In the silence that follows, the two poets stare awkwardly at their chewed fingernails, their hearts thudding in their chests, a little taken aback at how worked up they've become. Eventually, the Slam poet pipes up.

Well, he or she says with an air of finality, we're cooler.

Tim Clare is a writer, performer and poet. His first book, *We Can't All Be Astronauts*, won Best Biography/Memoir at the East Anglian Book Awards. His debut solo show, *Death Drive*, was hailed as 'the most compelling solo show on the Fringe' (WhatsOnStage).
> timclarepoet.co.uk

# ROOTS MANUVA'S ROMANTIC SOUL

Keats, Wordsworth and... Roots Manuva? David Barnes investigates the Romantic Rapper

Everybody thinks they know what the Romantic poets were all about – long, solitary walks through the Lake District, opium-induced visions, flouncy shirts and daffodils. Yet the ripples from Romanticism are far-reaching, and turn up in some unexpected places in modern society – most oddly, perhaps, in the lyrics of contemporary British rap artists. For me, the work of the rapper Roots Manuva provides the most perfect convergence of urban angst and Romantic lyric. As in the poetry of Wordsworth, Byron and Coleridge, Roots Manuva writes about negotiating and processing the self. One can see the same self-conscious, raw honesty – an honesty that is self-conscious because it's painfully aware that it reveals too much.

In contrast to the popular image of rap as violence, misogyny and bragging, the lyrics of Roots Manuva are complex and multi-layered. Roots (Rodney Smith, to give him his real name) was born in South London in 1972. He grew up in Stockwell, the son of a Pentecostal deacon and lay preacher, a family situation he has rapped about:

> I was raised in a Pentecostal church of God
> My father was the deacon, he used to stand preaching
> I used to steal collection, I used to catch a beating.
> ('Sinny Sin Sins' , 2001)

The track describes the young Roots questioning the authority of the Bible and struggling to be out of his father's shadow. Yet that sense of 'sinny sin sin' persists. The song identifies a split in the consciousness of the speaker. The speaker is both the young Roots/Smith, defiant towards the church's authority and rejecting the Christianity of the community he has been raised in, and the older man who claims to be 'far from a heathen'.

While the young Smith tries to make sense of a church where he's in 'the midst of the well-dressed/ talking 'bout singing, singing thanks and praise to the king of the Jews/' but which leaves him 'all confused', the older man reaches out to a God who can deliver from sin and its consequences: 'sins in your eye/ sin's gonna make you cry'. Even in an apparently straightforward song like 'Sinny Sin Sins' ('just a song of basic rhyme and reason'), it's clear that the narrator's relationship to his sense of self is far from easy.

In an interview, Smith has described his music as trying 'to contain aspects of egotistic-ness'. One can't help immediately jumping to Wordsworth, and John Keats's description of Wordsworth's poetry as the triumph of the 'egotistical sublime'. Keats's critique implies that Wordsworth makes his poetry serve some gigantic, all-seeing 'I', that the properties of inside and outside are dissolved in the advance of the giant Wordsworthian self.

But if Wordsworth was particularly prone to accusations of egotism, all Romantic poetry was concerned with *selfhood* and how to express it. While Wordsworth tended to stress the freedom of unbounded personal experience ('free, enfranchis'd and at large' he puts it in *The Prelude*), other Romantics provided a more complex, conflicted version.

Lord Byron both struggled with and profited from his own fame. His poetry feeds off his own 'Byronic' self-image; apparently providing a deeply raw autobiographical poetry, whilst holding this self-revelation at an ironic distance.[1]

In *Childe Harold's Pilgrimage*, Byron created a character that seems to be a thinly-veiled self-portrait. Childe Harold, like Byron, leaves England in bitter contempt and travels through Mediterranean Europe. He's on a quest to 'find himself'. But if Byron's original readers thought (and many did) that they were getting a picture of the poet himself, Byron made them think again.

In Canto III of the *Pilgrimage*, Byron himself breaks through the poetic narrative. The poet appears in the poem as an interrupting voice, tenderly mourning the loss of his daughter Ada after the break-up of his marriage. Here's the real deal, real flesh and blood, Byron seems to be saying. I hurt, I feel pain, he cries:

> Is thy face like thy mother's, my fair child!
> ADA! Sole daughter of my house and heart?
> When last I saw thy young blue eyes they smiled,
> And then we parted – not as now we part,
> But with a hope…

Byron is using his own rapidly growing notoriety as a tool to write poetry that apparently comes from the deepest heart. Byron depicts himself exiled over the waves, torn from his 'fair child'. This opening is vulnerable, sensitive. These lines shock the reader expecting a resumption of the story of Byron's 'Byronic' hero Harold. Instead they get – or seem to get – Byron himself looming suddenly out of the lyrics.

But in a sense, the 'real' Byron intervening is just another literary device, another game with the reader. We're left with an endless multiplicity of selves generating selves, all expressing an inward 'real' truth, all of them self-conscious literary devices.

I think that the rap lyrics of Roots Manuva do something similar. Roots has also self-consciously flirted with the Byronic image. In the video for his 2006 single 'Too Cold', he presents himself as 'Lord Manuval', a Byronic aristocrat living in a crumbling Gothic mansion with a host of courtesans. Roots lounges in a nightshirt, fights duels, and is pushed around in a bath chair. The mansion itself bears a striking resemblance to Newstead Abbey, the house Byron inherited when he was ten.

## Roots Manuva has self-consciously flirted with the Byronic image

Roots Manuva often raps about himself in the third person. 'A lot of people don't know 'bout Smith' he sings in 'Again and Again', and in 'Thinking' he begins 'I can't say what they want from Smith'. That track has a chorus which runs:

> Think about you, think about me
> Think about this, think about that
> I'm dangerously thinking
> Thinking about me sitting here thinking.
> ('Thinking')

Here, the mode of inward introspection typical of Romantic expression is given a further twist. Roots's persona in the song splits in two, as one half thinks about you and me, this and that, whilst another subject is able to think about the *original thinking self*: 'Thinking about *me sitting here thinking*'. Such games of subjectivity are possible only in a world that has shifted the goalposts, confused the relationship between persona and identity – in other words, a world of celebrity.

Roots gives us what we expect from a modern celebrity rapper: his ego. But instead of a brittle, macho persona, the words complicate the very nature of selfhood. Where is 'Roots' or 'Smith' located here? In the thinking self, in the thinking self thinking about the thinking self, or in the rapper rapping about the thinking self thinking about the thinking self? Again, the mantle of Romanticism is here in the inheritance of performative selfhood. I am who I am – but I'm not!

Root's rap lyrics have also always had a spiritual self-awareness. Partly this is a result of his Pentecostal inheritance; his language often seems to emerge directly from the black Pentecostal lexicon. Phrases like 'Let the spirit move you', 'revival', 'amazing grace', 'anointment' , 'the new man', 'righteousness', and 'repentance' scatter his lyrics.

To me this spiritual turn in the music has its own power, creating a dynamic that I continue to compare to Romantic poetry. It is interesting that the Pentecostal Church from which Rodney Smith emerges shares some of the same roots as Romanticism. Both have links to Methodism, and the theology of John Wesley. Pentecostalism develops Wesleyan theology – with its emphases on the 'higher light' and the spirit's emotive role in revival and conversion – and applies it to a highly theatrical, 'Spirit-led' style of worship.

The role of emotion in shaping Christian identity marks the lyrics of Roots Manuva. In the track 'All Things to All Men' (a collaboration with the group The Cinematic Orchestra) Roots seems to conflate the identity of the Christian believer with the loneliness of the creative genius. 'All things to all men' is a citation from St. Paul's first letter to the Corinthians, where the apostle writes: 'I am made all things to all men, that by all means I might save some'. Paul, as a Greek-speaking Jew, is able and willing to shift from one identity (Jewish) to another (Greek) in order that at all costs Christ's salvation might be preached.

Paul's gospel mission is transformed in Root's lyrics into the poetic task, as he raps out what he calls 'a heart felt recital/ from the wacky blacky man/ they should have called me Michael'. To identify with Michael Jackson here, as Roots does, is to identify with an oddball, a misfit.

This identification with Jackson acts as a prelude to his identification with Jesus Christ later in the song:

> We're searching for Jesus
> But I'll be damned if I'll be crucified
> By 10,000 spies
> Compulsive lies
> They hate me, they love me, they hate me

The New Testament's exhortation to follow Christ to his death is here mingled with a certain paranoia ('I'll be damned if I'll be crucified/ by 10,000 spies'), and signs of a kind of bipolar thinking ('they hate me, they love me').

Compare this with Coleridge's *Rime of the Ancient Marinere*:

> Alone, alone, all all alone,
> Alone on the wide wide Sea
> And Christ would take no pity on
> My soul in agony.

In both the invocation of Christ bursts strikingly through the words. But in neither does his appearance manage to deliver the protagonists from their plight. Whilst in Coleridge's poem it is the vision of nature and God reconciled that delivers the mariner, in Root's 'All Things to All Men', the hopes of spiritual freedom fail to make up for the pain and solitude experienced in the poem. 'I'm a *shackled* child singing the good song of freedom', Roots raps. While the 'good song of freedom' is sung, Roots is left shackled, chained.

Roots continues, crying that 'the pain never leaves', with 'tear drops dropping for the pain of the world'. 'Does God have a sense of humour?' he asks, before concluding that 'the joke's on us'. All this would seem like a general miserabilism, bemoaning the pain of humanity, were it not for Roots's constant return to his own self:

I don't wanna be alone
I'm born King so where's my throne
I'm too intense I'm too deep

Here, as I read it, the theological problems of evil and suffering are collapsed in on the problem of the ego. Specifically, Roots pleads the special case of genius – 'I'm born King'. But Roots is also 'too intense, too deep', returning us again to the central problem of Romanticism; it is a poetry of introspection that ultimately exiles the writer from his own creation. It's the old egotism again.

What changed with the Romantics was the increasing importance of putting yourself ('your *self*') out there. When John Donne wrote erotic love poems in the 17th century, people weren't really interested in whether they reflected lived experience because they were in a particular genre – they were love sonnets. The form was the thing, not the personality. By contrast, Byron and other's 'celebrity' fuelled constant speculation about the personal stories behind the radically self-orientated writing. But of course genuinely putting your self on display is impossible. Even the most nakedly autobiographical literary writing is still literary writing and, as such cannot be expected to represent an 'authentic' subjectivity. So the result – in the Romantics as in Roots Manuva – is a constantly shifting game of selfhood, of hiding and revealing. 'This is what me is' mumbles Roots at the end of Too

Cold, whose chorus – 'sometimes I love myself, sometimes I hate myself' – could have been the calling cry of the Romantic poets.

## a constantly shifting game of selfhood, of hiding and revealing

This game of distancing and focusing highlights the instability of the man Rodney Smith that the rapper Roots Manuva is rapping about. The self, 'Smith' is continually identified with then held at arm's length:

> Thirty years old and I never had a job
> Who's that layabout, professional slob
> Cooling in my yard eating corn on the cob
> Social scrounging, big time yob
> ('Thinking')

Beginning with honest angst associated with being in an artistic profession – 'thirty years old and I never had a job' – the song shifts narratorial position to an outside perspective: 'Who's that layabout, professional slob'. It's as if Roots, having given us his own inward insecurity, then shifts to occupying the position of a respectable bystander looking down on the wastrel Smith. This is repeated throughout the song: 'Cooling in my yard, eating corn on the cob' – first person narrative – then switches to that respectable person's condemnation of Smith: 'Social scrounging, big time yob'.

It's as if the very act of rapping – of forcing lyrics from your inner being – creates another self who looks down on and condemns the self-indulgent and irresponsible rapper. Yes, Roots gives us ego, but it's fractured, tortured ego. Roots Manuva creates a lyrical selfhood that is constantly shifting and unstable –a truth that the Romantics were the first to develop into poetic form.

## Notes

[1] This analysis of Byron is indebted to James Treadwell's very useful book, *Autobiographical Writing and British Literature*.

## Further reading / listening

Lord George Gordon Byron, *The Complete Poetical Works*, ed. Jerome McGann (Oxford: Oxford University Press, 1980-1993).

Roots Manuva, *Awfully Deep* (Big Dada, 2005).

Roots Manuva, *Run Come Save Me* (Big Dada, 2001).

Roots Manuva, *Slime and Reason* (Big Dada, 2008).

James Treadwell, *Autobiographical Writing and British Literature 1783-1834* (Oxford: Oxford University Press 2005).

William Wordsworth & Samuel Taylor Coleridge, *Lyrical Ballads*, ed. R.L. Brett & A.R. Jones (London: Methuen 1968).

William Wordsworth, *The Prelude: The Four Texts* (1798, 1799, 1805, 1850) (London: Penguin, 1995).

David Barnes was born in 1979. He read English at St Peter's College, Oxford before completing a PhD at Queen Mary, University of London on the work of Ezra Pound and John Ruskin. A writer and wandering academic, he has published essays and reviews in a number of places, including the Times Literary Supplement, Times Higher Education and Time Out. Alongside his interests in British hip-hop and poetry, David likes walking in East Sussex, travel and cooking.

# COMPOSING SPEECH

Hannah Silva on verbal music, talking backwards and the
art of double-tonguing

Composition is a way of thinking about how to organise material
- Jörg Lensing, 2009

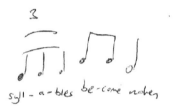

In daily life we are usually unaware of the musicality of speech. We don't
notice what range is used or the rhythms that are created. All of that becomes
habitual and exists only to support the meaning, or is the by-product of a
struggle to construct meaning. When we communicate with each other we
instinctively interpret a combination of semantics, intonation, rhythm, body
language and pragmatics.

Spoken word in performance can work with or against the habitual
musicality of language.

David Roesner describes how the application of compositional
tools and approaches to text, what he calls 'musicalization', allows us to
fully explore all aspects of text in performance:

Musicalization has re-introduced the full range of textual potential: as a rhythmical, gesticulatory, melodic, spatial and sounding phenomenon as well as a carrier of meaning (2008, p.50).

In this essay I analyse the ways in which I apply compositional tools and approaches within my own spoken word practice. I also explore the implications that this approach to creating and performing poetry might have on processes of writing, and on questions of meaning.

## Performance Poetry

In performance, several layers (the meaning of the words; the musicality of the delivery; the physicality of the performer) are perceived simultaneously.

Usually these layers describe each other, either instinctively, or in an attempt to add emphasis. Poets tend to illustrate the meaning of their words with movement, and with the use of voice, rather than treating these aspects as separate layers.

The musical term 'counterpoint' can be used to describe the interplay that occurs when these elements are treated separately. 'Counterpoint' describes melodic lines that follow parallel and contrary movements. In performance poetry this could be achieved literally, for instance, a recorded voice could work in counterpoint with a live voice. However it could also be explored in more complex ways, for instance, the intonation of spoken word could work in parallel and contrary movement to the expected intonation of the text, or the movement of the performer could be scored in parallel and contrary to the meaning of the words.

So, a poet could describe a beach ball in words but a bow and arrow with the body, then describe the sensation of walking in the sea in words while playing ball with the audience.

This compositional process is similar to orchestrating a symphony in which some parts carry melody, some rhythm, and combined they create harmony. There is a constant dialogue between instruments. The layers combine to make up the final composition.

In performance, the poet (whether consciously or not) works with language, music and the body simultaneously. An interdisciplinary process occurs within the performance poet, while a dialogic exchange takes place between poet and audience. This can give the impression of poetry being composed live in the space. As Joe Moran writes, 'Interdisciplinarity is always transformative in some way, producing new forms of knowledge in its engagement with discrete disciplines' (2002, p.16).

Rather than resulting in a sum of discrete elements, the interdisciplinary dialogue that takes place when the poet writes and performs poetry results in a new discipline. This discipline is what I refer to when using the label 'performance poetry'.

## Spracht komposition

Intonation = the melody, tone and intent of spoken language.

Michael Hirsch is a German composer and an exponent of *Spracht Komposition*.

There is no equivalent terminology to describe this form of vocal composition in English, I am translating it as 'composed speech'.

In *Lieder nach Texten aus dem täglichen Leben* (1992-95) Hirsch transcribed interviews from a television documentary, and notated every aspect of the spoken language - the hesitations in the speech, the coughs, the dynamics, the vocal noises that people make unconsciously. Then he re-composed the material, resulting in a text that sounds strangely like German, but is mostly impossible to understand (even for German speakers).

Elements of semantically intelligible language grow rampant from the thus developed abstract speech music, so that the act of listening sways back and forth between musical hearing to linguistic hearing, playing with comprehension and non-comprehension as well as with the boundaries between language and music (Hirsch, forthcoming 2011).

VORSPIEL

<ruhig und regelmässig>

NUUR
(schnä)
(ganselaach)
(sn)
(mm?)
CH,
kliklik
sischzndi
(maMIdüfdefde):

By using compositional tools, the layers within spoken word that are often unnoticed are revealed. Hirsch is not trying to conceal meaning, but to play with that border between meaning and sound, semantics and music. When working in this way, perhaps something can be revealed about the listener's attitude towards spoken word, the judgements made in response to accent, dialect, speech defects and hesitations. One compositional tool used by Hirsch is to reverse the sounds of language, not merely writing something backwards, but exploring vocally the process of reversing speech. This exercise re-confronts the performer and listener with the physiological challenge that we faced when learning to speak as children.

Some of my recent work took inspiration from *Spracht Komposition*. At a performance at London Word Festival (2010) I introduced myself in the following way:

> Hello, my name is Hannah, that's spelt H,A,N,N,A,H um...and... I live in Devon, with a dog, called Kibwe...that's K,I,B,W,E...um... Kibwe means blessed...in, Shona, I think, an.. African language coz he's a r...Rhodesian ridgeback...he's very big...um...and he's got a ridge, down his back...

A few days prior to the performance I recorded my first attempt at improvising this speech (nothing was written down). Then I learned the words, the intonation, the rhythm, the hesitations, the volume, the amount of breath used, the moments when my voice cracked... everything.

I take very small parts at a time. First I learn 'Hello' (repeat it twenty times until perfect) then 'Hello, my name is'...(repeat)....

Although I am working in a purely musical way, because this is my own natural, hesitant and self-conscious intonation, as soon as I begin, I also feel the corresponding emotions of self-consciousness and hesitancy, which is appropriate in the context of opening a performance. The principle is similar to the way (Stanislavskian) actors might create a precise physical score based on personal memory to help them access the emotions relevant to the script.

The restrictions of the precise score prevent me from over-acting and pushing my voice. I have to learn the speech well enough to be able to improvise with the order of the words while keeping the precision of the intonation. The intonation of the words is fixed, even when the order is different. After performing it straight, the introduction begins to break down into something like this:

Hello, my name is Shona, very big, um... and spelt Devon, that's H, A N N A N N um coz he's a r Rhodesian r rodes... very big um.... my name is, language, I think means blessed...

I am 'writing live', constructing new meanings by playing with the juxtaposition of words, phrases and sounds. The limitations of vocabulary and the precision of the intonation makes this a different approach to improvisation to that used in rap, hip hop, or devised theatre.

I experience a strange balance between being aware of constructing new meanings, while also working only with the musical layer of the speech. I find that if I become too aware of the meanings that I am constructing, I am more likely to trip up.

## The surface of language

These approaches to performing poetry mostly deal with what Tony Lopez calls 'the surface of the poem's language' (2006, p.3). Here Lopez discusses 'Innovative poetry in English':

> A key characteristic of this writing would be to focus our attention
> as readers onto language itself, rather than focusing on experience,
> as if language were merely a transparent medium (p.112).

'Language itself' could be explored on the page or in performance. Much poetry works with 'language itself' as well as meaning. But usually the language is composed in order to serve the meaning, and so might become 'transparent'.

One way to bring attention to language first and meaning second is to work against the natural melody of speech. For instance I could first learn the recognisable intonation of the phrase 'Ladies and Gentlemen, I'm delighted....' and then place that intonation onto other words (I've underlined the stresses):

Hello   my   nameisHan nah  thatsspeltH
Ladies  and  Gentleman  I'm delighted

and the other way around:

Ladies, & Gent le menI'm del   igh :ted...
Hello, my name is Hannah, that's spelt: H...

This (incredibly difficult to execute) collision of intonation against meaning completely disrupts the way in which the text is understood. Read against all the other layers of performance this might produce various interpretations.

# The collision of intonation against meaning disrupts the way in which text is understood

We are kept on the surface of the poem, looking at language and thinking about language and potential meaning; thinking about what meaning is and how language works[...]we are kept on the surface of the poem's language, not necessarily thinking about how language works in a generalised sense, but thinking about how these bits of language work together (Lopez, 2006, p.3).

Usually our intonation is transparent, which allows the listener to focus on meaning. By changing the intonation the listener is prevented from focusing on meaning first and delivery second. This kind of approach might be appropriate when the poet aims to play with elements of language in order to challenge notions of authorship, to deconstruct recognisable meaning, and to question language and meaning itself.

The composer Heiner Goebbels explains that when choosing a text to work with he not only looks at 'what they tell' but also 'how they tell':

> And if this question of 'how' has a musical dimension, like the rhythm in Gertrude Stein or the substantial reduction to single words in Heiner Müller, then I can work, then I have something to do, because I can make this syntax transparent. I can try to enlarge the view on the architecture of the text, to read the text with a magnifying glass. My interest is to share my observations with the reader or with the listener or, looking behind the author's way of writing, to show some of their writing strategies, to be able to understand more levels than just the overall semantic one (cited Gourgouris, 2004).

For Goebbels, every aspect of text - the punctuation, text layout, syntax, syllables - is relevant. Like Hirsch, Goebbels' approach reveals the layers at work within a text. Goebbels chooses texts which are appropriate for this way of working. While many writers punctuate to assist meaning, and in fact hope that the punctuation is not noticeable (or distracting), Stein questioned everything, making her writing particularly appealing to composers.

Forty percent of those with prosthetic limbs will go back into war. It's a positive thing.

Most of my work plays with two aspects of performance poetry: musicality of language, and meaning. You could say that disrupting the natural intonation of language disrupts meaning, brings the 'surface of language' to the foreground and confuses any intended message.

However, perhaps the opposite could also be true. By ignoring the meaning of a word/sentence/phrase, and working only with its musical properties, perhaps a deeper meaning is revealed.

We are accustomed to the news being delivered in a particular way, in a particular intonation and within a particular context.

If a sentence is taken out of that context and re-worked following some compositional strategies, perhaps the underlying meaning can be foregrounded, resulting in the message having greater impact than it would if delivered in either a dramatic way (voice trying to get a particular reaction) or a habitual way (the newsreader's intonation/the performance poet's typical delivery).

*Prosthetics* is built on one statement, taken from a pro-war U.S documentary:

Forty percent of those with prosthetic limbs will go back into war.

I also use the following sentences:

Amputation is the first step in rehabilitation. It's a positive thing.
A little girl cut the eye out and arm off her doll so that it would look like her father.

'It looks like a monster now', she said.

I began by recording a layer of vowel sounds taken from the initial line (forty percent...).When I repeat the sentence I miss off the first vowel sound, then the second, then the third, etc. Finally I reverse the order of the vowels. This sets up my backing rhythm over which I play with the other sentences, reversing the sounds:

> noitatupma is the first step, the first step in .... reha reha rehabilitation tion noit noit

A brief guide to speaking backwards: Record yourself speaking forwards, then reverse it on a computer, then play that back and learn it reversed, then record it reversed and reverse it again and check how close you are.

# when you speak backwards you reverse the physiological experience of speaking. You swallow words

Speaking backwards is not just a technical exercise; when you speak backwards you reverse the physiological experience of speaking. You swallow words. Consume your own speech. Amputate your own tongue, amputate your own ability to speak, distort yourself, amputate the words.

> reha rehabili bili ta tion...it's a positive thing...it's a, it's a...

At the end of the piece the full sentence emerges:

forty percent of those with limbs will go back into war
forty percent of those prosthetic limbs will go back into war
forty percent of with prosthetic limbs will go back into war
forty percent those with prosthetic limbs will go back into war
forty of those with prosthetic limbs will go back into war
forty percent of those with prosthetic limbs will go back into war

When playing with words as if they are musical building blocks, it's possible for the semantic meaning of individual words and sentences to be lost. However, when we talk about what a poem *means*, we are usually talking about the overall meaning - the theme, the metaphor, the implications, perhaps the message, perhaps the poet's intentions. This level of meaning can be served by the stylistic, compositional, and performance choices made by the poet, even when these choices are made in an effort to open up interpretation and prevent one overriding message from being communicated.

In *Prosthetics* I do not put forward my reaction or opinion on the issues. All of the material comes directly from the documentary. I play with sound, I play with voice, and I select the sentences that I feel needed to be given more attention.

Statements that were glossed over in the very positive and biased documentary are placed in a different context, and given time and space. In performance I amputate the words and sentences like the child in the documentary amputated her doll. This compositional approach allows more room for interpretation and reaction to the themes of the work.

## Sound Poetry: Threshold

In other cosmologies water is the primeval substance from which all forms come. The presence of water, thus, gives identity to the land (Norberg-Shultz, 1980, p.27).

The sensation of the tongue on the roof of the mouth. There's no breath left, but the sound continues. Articulations like insects dancing against teeth. Running into the space without words. Voice becomes running water. Water is the sound behind words.

What sounds does a human make? What is sound without the need for communication? Is there breath without thought? Is there poetry on the threshold of language? What is human sound before it reaches speech, identity, place? What is language at its beginnings? How does the human voice melt into the environment? Are there fricatives in the rush of water? Is there breath in the noise of air?

*Threshold* is a piece built on 'double tonguing' and sounds recorded on the moors in Devon. Double tonguing is an articulation technique I learnt over many years of playing the recorder.

It goes like this: dgdgdgddgdgdg. You can also work with triplets: dgd gdg dgd gdg. And other consonants: tktktktdiddleiddleiddleiddle

What makes sound poetry *poetry* and not music?

> Poetry implies subject matter; even when some particular work is wholly non-semantic, as in the microphonic vocal explorations of Henri Chopin, the non-semantic becomes a sort of negative semantics – one is conscious of the very absence of words rather than, as in vocal music, merely being aware of the presence of the voice (Higgins, 1980, online).

When performing *Threshold* there is none of the outward projection of energy that I usually experience when performing. My whole body listens, I am completely immersed in the physical experience of playing with sound.

Although I agree that when performing this piece at a poetry event, the 'absence of words' becomes present, and my practice is perceived as poetry, I think it is unnecessary and in this case impossible to draw lines between disciplines. That's not to say it's all a kind of creative mush, but that perhaps an interdisciplinary exchange is necessary to produce 'performance poetry', a discipline in itself.

When performing *Threshold*, I focus on the dialogue that occurs with the recorded sound, and with the space itself. The poet Sarah Hopkins wrote: 'It came over as the response of one body in nature to another, reminded me of how bird calls work' (personal communication, June 2009).

## Writing Sounds

Performance poetry... the performance of poetry... becomes exciting when the audience witnesses poetry being created in front of them (or around them or behind or above them). Every layer of performance becomes a part of the work, every listener plays a part in the composition.

After exploring these approaches to composing text, my perception of language begins to shift. I become more aware of the inherent musicality of language; words become building blocks, like notes. I notice how many syllables a word contains and am able to play words like music... two syllable words become couplets, three syllable words become triplets... and I realise that there is more to language than meaning.

## Further reading

D. Higgins, 'A Taxonomy of Sound Poetry', http://www.ubu.com/papers/Higgins_sound.html.

Michael Hirsch, *Lieder Nach Texten aus dem Täglichen Leben* (Berlin: Edition Juliane Klein, 2002).

Michael Hirsch, 'Theatre in Small quantities – on composition for speech, sound and objects' in. David Roesner & M. Rebstock (eds.), *Composed Theatre: Aesthetics, Practices and Processes* (Bristol: Intellect, forthcoming 2011).

Jorg Lensing, Speaking at: David Roesner & M. Rebstock, *Processes of devising composed theatre* (AHRC funded conference, Exeter University).

Tony Lopez, *Meaning Performance* (Cambridge: Salt, 2006).

J. Moran, *Interdisciplinarity*. (London and New York: Routledge, 2002).

C. Norberg-Schulz, *Genius Loci. Towards a Phenomenology of Architecture* (New York: Rizoli, 1980).

David Roesner, 'The polyphony of performance: Musicalization in contemporary German Theatre', *Contemporary Theatre Review*, 18:1, pp. 44-55.

David Roesner, *Processes of Devising Composed Theatre* (Exeter, 2009).

Hannah Silva is a playwright, performance poet and theatre maker, known for vocal gymnastics and linguistic experiments. She composes speech, choreographs language, and exploits 'double tonguing' to create a unique form of spoken word performance. > hannahsilva.co.uk

# RADIO AND...

A radio-fiction essay: James Wilkes sends test
transmissions from an underground bunker

| FX | *HISS OF RADIO STATIC. THE RADIO IS TUNED – AN OLD ANALOGUE DIAL. RISING OUT OF THE FUZZ, THE OUTLINES OF TWO HUMAN VOICES* |
|---|---|
| JAMES | ...poetry reading based on the idea of apocalypse, which we called 'I am the last man alive'. |
| HOLLY | Because there were three of us and two of us weren't men. |
| JAMES | Exactly. We gave ourselves these biographies which were based on the plots of disaster films, you know those ones where only one man survives, so Abi was, I think she was – what's the film with Denzel Washington? |
| HOLLY | The Book of Eli. |
| JAMES | Yeah, she was that one. And you were The Day After Tomorrow and I was I Am Legend. We were imagining what poetry might come out of a post-apocalyptic movie. |

| | |
|---|---|
| HOLLY | Yeah, a mutated hybrid monster. And growing out of that, we decided to take it further, and the aspect we really liked from that reading was radio. The radio voice. |
| JAMES | The ruined voice. |
| HOLLY | Yeah, it seemed to us that radio and ruin went together somehow. And we'd also got into Numbers Stations, panic broadcasts. All that kind of end of the world stuff. So we started collaborating, trying out new procedures and experimenting with a kind of radiophonic poetry, and eventually we had an hour of material... |
| FX | *STATIC INTERFERENCE WASHES LOUDER. THE RADIO IS SWITCHED OFF* |
| JAMES | And now we're here. In a disused transmission bunker. Which is perfect, because Holly's work is really suited for radio actually. It's already a radio voice. Because of the way |
| FX | *HOLLY COUGHS* |
| JAMES | she begins with a cough. Or with a breath |
| FX | *HOLLY BREATHES IN* |

JAMES            or

FX _____ *HOLLY BUMPS THE MICROPHONE*

HOLLY            sorry everyone

JAMES            or a bump against the microphone. Seeking out
                 moments of trespass. That's what Steven Connor talks
                 about.

HOLLY            Does he?

JAMES            Yeah, he calls it accidental trespass. When the
                 unensouled breaks through into ensouled sound.
                 Which is what happens with a cough. In Aristotle's
                 terms, anyway. But what you do, it's not accidental.
                 We're talking deliberate trespass here. With intent.

HOLLY            Thanks.

JAMES            But radio actually needs that, you know. A radio voice
                 is only a voice if it sounds. In fact it's only radio if it
                 sounds. That's why dead air is such bad manners.

HOLLY            Yes - because it obliterates the radio, and the whole –
                 the whole apparatus of society

FX _____ *STATIC FUZZ FADES IN*

ORSON WELLES      This is Orson Welles, out of character, to tell you ... we annihilated the world before your very ears and utterly destroyed the CBS...

FX          *FUZZ FADES OUT*

JAMES        Exactly. The ball disappears under a blanket, and like Piaget's child, we're never quite sure that it's going to return. Until it does. To keep it going, to keep the ball in the air, the radio voice can't afford to make, you know, nice distinctions.

HOLLY        The rustle of papers in a studio is enough. A cough or a breath is enough.

JAMES        Yeah. And so there's fear. From the start there's fear.

HOLLY        There's plenty of that down here. Like a warren of underground tunnels and then this little booth at the end of it. But why don't we just play the tapes we brought?

JAMES        OK. Sure. Let's play the tapes. Here we go.

HOLLY        Hang on, not that –

FX          *EMERGENCY TONE*

TAPE VOICE    Remember this. Frequency. Calling me. May Day.

Mayday. Help me. Heap me. Remember my coordinate. It's. No cure no cure. No cure. No cure no cure. No cure.

| | |
|---|---|
| _FX_ | _CUTS_ |

HOLLY          OK we're back.

JAMES          Right. OK. Sorry, looks like I hit the wrong... hang on. Button. Right. OK? OK, here we go.

NARRATOR       Radio and fear are entwined. Even if the breath is there, there's still fear. Fear of the headlines in that momentary intake before the newsreader speaks. And also at that same moment relief; relief which accuses, because whatever is about to be announced, the fact that you're hearing it on the radio probably means it hasn't happened to you. Radio: the medium of disaster, the relay of disaster and the propagation of suffering.

| | |
|---|---|
| _FX_ | _MORSE TAPPING_ |

NARRATOR       It blossomed as the Titanic sank beneath the sea. And since that day, radio has been making the disaster immaterially present, instantly, all around the world. When Walter Benjamin made a radio broadcast for children about the Lisbon earthquake of 1755, he warned against overdoing the reportage of destruction, saying that "to hear all of this and nothing else would please no-one." And yet his piece is as full of dreadful eyewitness accounts of carnage as any 24-hour news channel today.

JAMES    [OVER NARRATOR] How can we deal with that? That radio exploits the disaster?

HOLLY    [OVER NARRATOR] Well we can't just ignore this material. And it is material. You can't pretend it's not there.

JAMES    [OVER NARRATOR] Yeah, and you can't pretend to be faithful to it either. Like the dog listening to his master's voice from the grave. It doesn't wash.

HOLLY    [OVER NARRATOR] It's just melancholia. It has to be worked on.

NARRATOR    And even before the Titanic, as early as 1902, radio was said to be creating "ghostlands" and "dreamlands". Creating echoing counter-worlds of desire and fear. Behind it the concept of the ether, a kind of sublime recording medium which might contain the traces, however diminished, of every voice which ever transmitted, every packet of information sent out into the vast sidereal space of the universe, drifting forever until it might at last dock in another soul.

HOLLY    [OVER NARRATOR] It's all getting a bit... can we turn it off for a while?

JAMES          [OVER NARRATOR] Yeah.

<u>FX</u>              <u>*NARRATOR CUTS*</u>

JAMES          I know what you mean. And is it just me or is it getting
               a bit warm down here?

HOLLY          No, it is. They said the ventilation systems had been
               playing up the last few days. We're getting through it
               though. That's SETI, spiritualism and Kittler covered.

JAMES          Well you're more into that than me. Do you mean about
               playing the um, the coronal suture with a gramaphone
               needle, in that Rilke story that Kittler mentions?

HOLLY          Ooh, I'd forgotten that one. The white noise of the
               skull. No, I was thinking about the guy who creates a
               death mask of Goethe's vocal chords, and then picks
               up the resonances of his voice from the wooden panels
               of his parlour.

JAMES          Nice. And you do get this, don't you, with radio, its
               past continually interrupting its present.

HOLLY          It seems to. It might be something to do with ether, like
               the narrator was saying.

| | |
|---|---|
| JAMES | Yes, it's amazing what a persistent idea that is. Lord Reith was talking about it still in 1924, even though it had gone out of the window as a kind of scientific plausible substance with Einstein. |
| HOLLY | That's probably because it's such a powerful idea. It just migrates sideways from science into popular culture. And speaking of Steven Connor like we were, didn't he write something about Einstein saying that ether had animated what was previously inert space... |
| JAMES | ...making the idea of relativity thinkable in the first place. Mmm. Einstein mentioned something like that in a piece he wrote for the New York Times I think in 1929, that the invention of ether had brought space to life. And you're into physicists too, aren't you? Jocelyn Bell. |
| HOLLY | Yes. She discovered pulsars. |
| JAMES | Which are what exactly? |
| HOLLY | They're – they're radio pulses made by dead stars that have been knocked off their axis. |
| FX | *REGULAR TICKING* |
| HOLLY | They transmit this energy like a lighthouse, going round and round and round. And they're incredibly |

regular. As in atomic clock regular. So in 1967 you've got Joceyln Bell, who's a PhD student at the time, and she's going through the data that's coming in from a radio telescope, and she sees this signal. Tick tick tick. So regular she thinks it must be interference from earth, and she starts to label it 'scruff' on her charts. Then, later on, she puts another note next to it. LGM.

JAMES            What did that stand for?

HOLLY            Little Green Men.

JAMES            Seriously? You mean ET was calling her?

HOLLY            Well no, and I think it was kind of tongue in cheek at the time. But it was really baffling. And then a few years later they work out it's a pulsar, a rotating neutron star, and her supervisor gets a Nobel prize.

JAMES            Her supervisor?

HOLLY            That's science for you.

FX               *TICKING STOPS*

JAMES            And you've taken this on, haven't you, this notion of scruff.

HOLLY            I'm a scruff poet.

JAMES          Yeah. I really like that. Because you've got this play
               between scruff as meaningless interference and the
               kind of animating pulse that might indicate intelligent
               life. And you've also said, 'scruff can be scratches or
               fluff'. So you've got scratches -

HOLLY          Hang on Jamie, I'm just being told, the producer is
               saying something in my ear about the studio being...
               no, no it's not. [PAUSE] No, sorry, carry on.

JAMES          Being what?

HOLLY          Nothing. They just thought there was some problem
               with the ducts or something, but I'm being told it's OK
               now.

JAMES          Shall I carry on?

HOLLY          Yes. Yes carry on.

JAMES          OK. So these scratches score across the pre-recorded
               surface and provide a measure of a record's life, the
               material history if you like of one particular instance of
               sound. And then you've got fluffs, and – are you OK?

HOLLY          Yeah, fine. It's just gone a bit quiet. In my ear. They're
               usually taking readings and chatting away.

JAMES          Is it their lunchbreak?

HOLLY          Probably. Sorry – fluffs.

JAMES          OK, fluffs, so: these are unique to live performances
               right, the stumble, or the, the tickle at the back of the
               throat that demands to be cleared. You begin with a
               cough, with a breath, live on air. And radio begins, and
               its history begins, all over again.

HOLLY          Well that kind of thing's an antidote to the bunker
               mentality. The fact that we're there, with our bodies,
               in front of people, being radio voices but with bodies
               attached.

JAMES          Yeah. I was thinking we could build a machine though,
               a kind of hand-cranked transmitter...

HOLLY          Like two mad professors?

JAMES          Yes, and we could both be cranking the handles, like
               two Igors maybe, and slowly this transmitter would
               power up, and all these radios around the room would
               pick up our voices and that would be the reading.

HOLLY          Sounds good. Let's do it.

JAMES          Because right now we're here, and actually this studio
               they're letting us use is a really interesting space, you

were telling me it was actually a genuine cold war bunker

HOLLY          down below the Northern Line

JAMES          and some of the tapes they've got still in the machines, it's quite amazing. Quite creepy really.

HOLLY          But this is what I mean about the bunker mentality, it can get claustrophobic. And I think that's one of the reasons you're interested in dreamlands. They're the opposite pole. You make the connection to Dreamland which was the name of a funfair in Margate in one of your poems don't you?

JAMES          Well it's part of a complex of ideas I'm interested in but I haven't managed to disentangle yet. It's about different kinds of utopias...

HOLLY          And radio is one, and I guess that mass leisure is another.

JAMES          Yeah, in both of them there's that surrealist idea of the power of dreams and desire to transform everyday life when they precipitate in concrete objects. And Benjamin picks up on this when he writes about the revolutionary energies of the outmoded.

HOLLY          Though in funfairs that possibility is tamed. You write

'Dreamland was a controlled explosion'.

JAMES          And the same's true of radio. I mean let's roll some of
               these old tapes – all you'll get is an earful of encryption
               and paranoia.

FX             *CLUNK THEN HISS OF TAPE STATIC*

HOLLY          But behind it there's still that utopian possibility.

JAMES          Yeah and beyond it, outside the crypt. There's a whole
               other architecture of airy towers and pylons sketched
               against the sky and... um...

HOLLY          What?

JAMES          Turn around, I thought I just saw something outside
               the -

FX             *A SUDDEN THUMP, THEN SEVERAL MORE, AS*
               *SAFETY GLASS SLOWLY SPLINTERS*

HOLLY          Oh God, what is that?

JAMES          It's breaking the glass -

FX             *CHAIRS PUSHED BACK. BUMP AGAINST THE MIC*

HOLLY          Quick, this way. There's another door.

FX                    *MORE THUMPS, THEN CRASH OF GLASS. HEAVY*
                      *FOOTSTEPS, THEN THE MIC IS KNOCKED HARD*
                      *AND GOES DEAD. SILENCE. THE TAPE HISS*
                      *GROWS*

TAPE VOICE            [CALM, EVEN, UNINFLECTED] touch-type entry
                      lebanon entry guarantee retouched accounts portugal
                      handle biafra accounts caritas knightsbridge accounts
                      note-take duplicate lebanon entry touch-type manilla
                      entry knightsbridge note-take olivetti wire

FX                    *TAPE HISS CONTINUES. TAPE CLICKS TO A STOP.*
                      *SILENCE.*

*END TRANSMISSION.*

## Further reading

Walter Benjamin, 'Surrealism: The Last Snapshot of the European Intelligentsia', in Michael W. Jennings, Howard Eiland & Gary Smith (eds.), *Selected Writings, Vol. 2* (Cambridge, MA: Harvard University Press, 1999), pp. 207-221.

Walter Benjamin, 'The Lisbon Earthquake', in *Selected Writings, Vol. 2* (Cambridge, MA: Harvard University Press, 1999), pp. 536-540.

Steven Connor, ''Transported Shiver of Bodies': Weighing the Victorian Ether' (2004). Available online at: http://www.stevenconnor.com/ether.

Steven Connor, 'Whisper Music' (2007). Available online at: http://www.bbk.ac.uk/english/skc/whispermusic.

Friedrich Kittler, *Gramaphone, Film, Typewriter*, trans. Geoffrey Winthrop-Young & Michael Wutz (Stanford: Stanford University Press, 1999).

John Durham Peters, *Speaking into the Air: A History of the Idea of Communication* (Chicago: University of Chicago Press, 1999).

Jeffrey Sconce, *Haunted Media: Electronic Presence from Telegraphy to Television* (Durham, NC: Duke University Press, 2000).

Orson Welles, *The War of the Worlds* (New York: Columbia Broadcasting Service, 1938).

James Wilkes has been collaborating with Holly Pester on a series of poetic texts exploring the radio voice since May 2010. He has also collaborated with artists Townley and Bradby and The Wayward Plant Registry, and with Dr Louise Whiteley to write *Interior Traces*, a live radio play about brain imaging. His poetry has been published by Penned in the Margins and Veer.

> renscombepress.co.uk

# ENJOYING AND EXAMINING POETRY

Poems and pedagogy? Alex Runchman offers a teacher's perspective

Which poems in the *AQA English Literature Anthology* did you most enjoy?

Compare your enjoyment of 'Catrin' by Gillian Clarke with one poem by Seamus Heaney and two poems from the Pre-1914 Poetry Bank.

Remember to compare   —   the content of the poems
                       —   the ways the poems are written

This question appeared on the AQA GCSE English Literature Exam of June 2008. Ostensibly it gives students free rein to write about those characteristics of the poems in their prescribed anthologies that they find most engaging: a gift. In practice, however, it is a disaster: the kind of question most likely to spawn clichéd answers about how 'good' the use of alliteration is in a particular poem, how the enjambment creates 'an interesting effect', or how childhood is 'an important theme'.

This question from the Irish Leaving Certificate Exam (the equivalent of British A-Levels) for the same year is even worse. For 20 marks (10% of the entire paper):

Did you enjoy reading ['Phenomenal Woman' by Maya Angelou]?
Write a piece where you give your response to this question.

Although it is perhaps better than the alternative ('If you were to write a poem entitled 'Phenomenal Man', what qualities would you give that man?'), the question allows responses that might be perfectly truthful (and valid) but which say nothing at all about the student's understanding of it as a poem: 'I enjoyed it because it reminds me of my Mum' or 'I didn't like it because I think the poet sounds up herself'.

The question is from the 'Ordinary Level' paper, but those on the 'Higher Level' aren't much better: 'Write an essay outlining your reasons for liking/not liking Larkin's poetry?' or 'Does the poetry of Adrienne Rich speak to you?' Perhaps the greatest gripe for the poetry lover is that all of these questions more or less invite students to answer 'I didn't enjoy reading this poem because I don't like reading poetry.' Or to make them think that just because they didn't enjoy 'Catrin' by Gillian Clarke, or because Adrienne Rich didn't 'speak' to them, that all other poetry must therefore be dead to them too.

The kicks you can get out of tearing such questions to shreds are ultimately limited. But their emphasis on enjoyment draws attention to a fundamental paradox in the way that poetry is taught in secondary schools and also in the way that it is perceived beyond the classroom. On the one hand, poetry is meant to be fun. Daisy Goodwin thinks so, Neil Astley thinks so, and there is a growing market for live poetry, so why should anyone suggest otherwise? It is democratic, inclusive, reaching out to an

**poetry is meant to be fun.
Daisy Goodwin thinks so,
Neil Astley thinks so**

audience. Equally, though, poetry is difficult. What T. S. Eliot said was a necessary condition only of Modernist poetry has generally been taken to apply to all poetry written before and since. But what is most often forgotten is that being difficult does not prevent a poem from also being enjoyable. In some cases the difficulty is actually part of the enjoyment. It is also true that difficulty is no indication of a poem's worth: many very simple poems are very good and many very difficult poems are very bad. The trap that teachers tend to fall into is either over-emphasising the difficulty to the extent that poetry becomes inaccessible to students, or over-emphasising the entertainment with the consequence that poetry becomes trivialised.

Once you start probing it, 'poetry' becomes a fairly unhelpful blanket term that covers a great range of different kinds of writing in verse. But I believe that your chances of enjoying poetry, *all* poetry, or at least of judging whether it's any good or not, are going to be higher if you can acquire an appreciation of how rhyme, rhythm, metaphor and so on work. This needn't be any more difficult than learning the basic vocabulary and grammar of a language.

But one of the problems, in my experience, is that many teachers do not have a confident grasp of the basic techniques of poetry; many teachers, given the questions above, would say that they don't enjoy reading poetry themselves and would simply prefer for it not to be on the syllabus. It's too specialised. Even amongst my fellow English PhD students, those who are embarking upon careers in literature, there are several who describe themselves as 'not a poetry person' and who point out that nobody ever taught them 'the nuts and bolts' of poetry (as with language learning, it becomes more daunting as you grow older). If they are so wary, how can we expect school kids to get excited about it?

The ways in which you first encounter poetry (and the kinds of poem you encounter) make a lasting impression. We all engage with poetry in the nursery rhymes and games of earliest childhood, but it is in the classroom that most of us acquire a sense of poetry as something crafted; it is in the classroom that we are either inspired or put off for life. I would bet that more people remember the poems they disliked at school than the ones they enjoyed. In my own case, I long harboured a grudge against Gerard Manley Hopkins because I once got a detention for failing to learn 'Pied Beauty'. Getting kids to learn poems is considered a no-no in today's needs-sensitive climate because it's humiliating for those who simply can't remember. But this ignores the fact that you might learn a poem for pleasure and not just to be tested on it later.

There's no doubt that poetry teaching is now more inventive and creative than it used to be: no more simply reading, memorising and doing comprehension questions on Romantic and Victorian classics you're too young to appreciate. But all of the innovation is undermined when the teachers are so ill-equipped to tackle poetry themselves and when the whole enterprise of learning leads to writing formulaic essays for exams.

Most schools include poetry modules in Year 7 which, at best, encourage students to play with words and write their own verse, whilst also introducing them to a few technical features, forms, and a range of contemporary and long-established poems. The kind of thing that works is giving students the words of an actual poem jumbled up and asking them to use the words to write their own pieces. Not only does this enable them to produce creative works of their own, it also means that when they read the original they are better able to understand the kinds of decision that the poet had to make in writing it.

Increasingly, schools are inviting real live poets and self-proclaimed wordsmiths to give special workshops, or encouraging students to take part in youth slams and 'word offs'. This is all great, demonstrating that poetry is alive and, in many cases, deserving of performance. It needs to be handled with care, however. You don't want to create the impression that the only poetry worth listening to is what works well in performance, and you need to teach students to be critical as well as enthusiastic. Enabling them to relate what they read to their own experience is crucial, but excessive attempts to make poetry seem cool are likely to backfire. By the time they reach GCSE, most students are much too savvy to believe that Carol Ann Duffy is worth reading simply because she writes about sex.

The key thing is that students discover how language and poetic craft work for themselves. It's like learning a language – you'll learn quicker if you're immersed in a society that only speaks that language rather than if you are merely told the technical aspects in a classroom. It's futile to keep explaining what an iambic pentameter is, and clapping out the beats, unless students have a chance to try writing iambic pentameters of their own. I suspect that you can't really get to grips with poetry unless you've made a serious enough attempt at writing

## it's like learning a language

it yourself. Your own poetry doesn't have to be any good – and, in fact, the worse it is the more you are likely to appreciate a poem that succeeds in expressing what you couldn't express yourself. And there's no accounting for the degree of inspiration that distinguishes a really good poem from one that is merely technically competent.

At worst, these Year 7 modules involve students going through poems by, say, Kit Wright with highlighter pens to mark nouns, verbs and adjectives; answering prompts that begin 'I like this poem because...'; brainstorming 'interesting descriptive words'; and doing Wikipedia research homework on poets whose poems they never actually read. Considering that this is one of the few points in most students' secondary school careers when they are not working towards tests or examinations, this kind of proto-GCSE preparation is particularly disheartening. One of the joys of teaching poetry to twelve and thirteen year olds is that they tend to have relatively few preconceptions. I especially remember a class in which a reluctant twelve-year-old pointed out that each of the stanzas of William Carlos Williams's 'The Red Wheelbarrow' –

so much depends
upon

a red wheel
barrow

glazed with rain
water

beside the white
chickens –

actually looked like a wheelbarrow on the page, the longer first line as the handle and the shorter second one the wheels. Asking students to write their own poems exactly mimicking Williams's structure was also productive, the most perceptive of them noticing, as well as the three-word one-word pattern, that 'wheelbarrow' and 'rainwater' are compound words broken up by the line breaks and coming up with compounds of their own. On first encountering the poem, most students had assumed it was 'not proper poetry'; but by having a go at something similar themselves they began to appreciate its artistry.

Poetry probably suffers most in schools in the build up to GCSEs with the introduction of the dreaded anthology. The problem is not so much with the poems themselves as with the functions they are made to perform – essentially as gauges of a student's ability to compare and contrast, to spot themes and so on. Any teacher who teaches specifically for the exam – particularly during the early stages of the course when it isn't strictly necessary – is condemning his or her class to mind-numbingly dull lessons. The most dispiriting one I ever saw was taught by a County Council adviser sent round to schools to deliver the party line on how it ought to be done. She chose a standard GCSE question and then put up a 'funky' table on an overhead projector (yes, that is an oxymoron: beware any teacher who describes their lessons, and especially their tables or worksheets, as 'funky', 'jazzy', or – god forbid – 'sexy') with boxes for 'themes', 'images', 'techniques' and 'language'. Into these boxes students put points about the poems they were going to compare. She then circulated the mark scheme for how to get a C or above, which students had to highlight. Then they got an example of a C grade essay which they also had to highlight. You could have sat through the lesson without realising that she was talking about poetry at all. All the enjoyment that other teachers had tried to foster in earlier years had been lost.

## beware any teacher who describes their lessons as 'funky', 'jazzy', or - god forbid - 'sexy'

It does make sense that contemporary poets should be prioritised in the exam. After all, they engage most closely with a world familiar to the students. But the quartet of Heaney, Clarke, Duffy and Armitage is rather conservative. Additionally, many of the 'Poems from Other Cultures' are there because they address 'issues' rather than for their poetic value. But it is the 'pre-1914 Poetry Bank' that most skews perspective with its impression that all poetry written before 1914 can be neatly grouped together and therefore that there's not really much difference between, say, Shakespeare and Browning. The generic question on the Literature paper asks students to compare poems by Heaney and Clarke or Duffy and Armitage with two of the pre-1914 poems in 45 minutes. In practice, only four of the pre-1914 poems are ever studied in any detail, which means that Jonson and Browning are doing well if they get two sentences each in any given essay, whilst it is unusual for Wordsworth or Tennyson to be read at all. The fact that a student might then go on to study Duffy's *The World's Wife* at A-Level means that even students who reach this stage may leave school having had a very limited exposure to different poets.

This presents a catch-22 scenario because you can't do away with exams and you do need some kind of a framework to show why one response is more sophisticated than another. But the fact remains that every year students go through the system knowing that if they can master techniques for answering exams and meeting all the assessment objectives they can do well without engaging with the texts much at all.

When I taught A-Level, intelligent students would commonly ask me 'Do you think my essay's got enough AO4 in it?' rather than 'Do you think my argument's convincing?' or 'Am I justified in making such and such a point?' It's exam-machine thinking and the curriculum encourages it. The examiners who set the questions I derided at the beginning of this piece would insist that they promote 'differentiation by outcome' (teaching jargon for 'the strongest candidates, who will understand what is expected of them, will answer best'). This can't be denied, but does it mean that they're better readers of poetry or just better at answering exam questions? And whilst we're back on those questions, what are we to make

## do you think my essay's got enough AO4 in it?

of the fact that every student who answers them positively vindicates the whole GCSE syllabus? Hey, even if they only get an E, at least they enjoyed reading 'Catrin' by Gillian Clarke. What would happen if one year the exam asked

> 'Which poems in the *AQA English Literature Anthology* did you least enjoy?'

I don't pretend to have a solution. But I used to wonder why there was so little poetry written specifically for teenagers when fiction sales for this age group have stratosphered – *Harry Potter*, Pullman's *Dark Materials* Trilogy and *Twilight*, whatever you may think of them, are only the most obvious examples. I now think it has something to do with the fact that poetry can't rely upon plot and character, which are the propelling forces of all the teen lit I have read. Nonetheless, I'd like to see more poets try to write for teens. Perhaps Duffy and Armitage are in fact the closest we currently have (though I suspect most teenagers would find someone like Patience Agbabi much cooler).

If I am sure about anything it's that if students are going to enjoy poetry they're going to have to learn to accept that it will always be open to many interpretations and that there can never be a definitive meaning – the old Keatsian 'negative capability' chestnut. If you 'get' a work of literature first time there's no reason ever to reread it and it becomes pointless. You might as well forget it. The 'fill in the tables' approach to GCSE teaching works completely against this openness of interpretation. I am also sure that the poetry students will most enjoy will be the poetry they have discovered for themselves, rather than works that they have had shoved down their throats. The best teachers are facilitators, exposing students to as wide a range of works as possible but not over-directing their responses.

One of the most heartening moments of my career as a secondary school English teacher came some time after I had left the job in order to return to academia. I received an email from a former student whom I had taught up to GCSE. She had been one of my more able and independent-minded students, but she had also been sceptical of most of the poetry on the course. This is what she wrote:

> John Milton. Why, just why, are we not taught about him when he writes the most sublime, beautiful poetry there is? He is, just, wow. How on earth can someone write a 10,000 line poem, in perfect iambic pentameter, juxtaposed so it appears just like a story, that has vivid imagery but is still easy to empathise with, in a truly flawless way - and do all this while BLIND? I am truly astounded by it.

I can't emphasise enough how spirit-raising and cynicism-conquering such enthusiasm can be for a teacher of poetry. You have something to work with. I think I'd have been happier if she hadn't mentioned the iambic pentameter and made that slightly confused point about juxtaposition – it sounds a bit too much like exam speak. But all the same, this says more to me about her enjoyment of poetry than any answer she might have written for her GCSE exam. I am confident enough that this is a student who will now continue to read Milton, to read poetry, and to seek out more; and that is about as much as any poetry teacher can hope for.

Alex Runchman is studying for a PhD at Trinity College Dublin on the American writer Delmore Schwartz. He was formerly a secondary school teacher in Oxfordshire, and has also taught English as a foreign language in several countries.

# THE LINE[1]

What is the poetic line and how do you write it? Katy
Evans-Bush walks the high wire

> It is as if we were back at the *Théâtre des Funambules*, during the
> era of *Les Enfants du Paradis*, when pale-faced Pierrots walked a
> rope before stepping onto the stage. It was actually a tightrope
> set across the proscenium, in front of Harlequin's coat (the stage
> curtain). Actors who were not acrobats or mimes fell off the rope
> and were sent to perform far up backstage. So the word 'rope' was
> banned from the theatre and its use subject to a fine. One had to
> say 'line'.
>
> Marcel Marceau, Foreword to *On the High Wire* by Philippe Petit[2]

A book fell into my hands last Christmas Eve: a loan from a friend who used
to be a circus performer. It is out of print, almost as hard to obtain as the
condition it describes: *On the High Wire*, by Philippe Petit, translated by Paul
Auster, with a foreword by Marcel Marceau. The book doesn't mention Petit's famous walk between the towers of the World Trade Center, but focuses
instead on the technique of wire-walking, great walkers who have mastered
it, and the spiritual impulse and rigour of the walk. It is the most natural
thing in the world to get ideas about how to approach the writing of poetry
from these great silent masters. They are dedicated to the line, subjugated to
the illusion, and dependent for their own lives on their discipline.

    A poet is not going to die if his line is slack or unsupported. But
his volition and his meaning – which are the same, for the duration of the

## the line must be taut, and strong enough to hold

poem, as his existence – will. The line must be taut, and strong enough to hold, and the grease left over from production must not be oozing out of its 'soul'. (Petit buys huge lengths of cable and leaves them out in the garden for 'several years' to become completely dry and weathered, then cleans them with gasoline. Elizabeth Bishop did the same with her poem drafts.)

It's not enough just to walk the line: the art depends on a daily familiarity with it. 'Whoever intends to master the art of walking on them,' Petit writes, 'must take on the task of seeking them out. Of comparing them. Of keeping those whose properties correspond to his aspirations. Of learning how to knot them. Of knowing how to tighten them. It is the work of a lifetime.'

Later he writes, 'If you want the High Wire to transform you into a high-wire walker you must discover the classic purity of this game. But first you must master its technique. Too bad for the one who turns it into a chore.'

Here I need to make a similar disclaimer to that made by Don Paterson in his two-part essay, 'The Lyric Principle',[3] where he defines his subject, lyric poetry, as 'that aspect of the art that concerns itself to its music, i.e. to the patterning of its sounds.' Where Paterson says that 'language itself has a lyric basis and is itself a poetic system, and that poetry is merely the natural result of language placed under certain kinds of formal pressure and emotional urgency,' he is talking about one cross-section – sound, as expressed in vowels and consonants. We are occupying ourselves here with another of the almost limitless cross-sections available: the line. Clearly the line plays a different role in sound, concrete, 'innovative,' 'post-avant,' language and other poetries. But our working definition is still very broad, and ranges across styles and eras, and even widely differing sets of intentions. It includes, in part, many of the poetic styles listed above, and certainly applies to something like, say, Edwin Morgan's 'Siesta of a Hungarian Snake.'

The line is not the destination. Although its anchoring points – the nearest it has to a geography – are of the utmost importance, they are not the destination. They are more like the points of a compass. The real destination, in poetry as well as the Funambules, is what you do while you're up there. The line must hold you up so you can do it. Here is that snake poem in its entirety:[4]

s sz sz SZ sz SZ sz ZS zs Zs zs zs z

A line of poetry, whether 'free' or 'formal' (more on that later), is made – crudely – of words and line endings. Words are made of meaning and sound. Meaning is made of dictionary definitions, association, history, etymology, and even – to some extent – sound. This can be based on onomotapeia, as Morgan demonstrates, or can be more expressionist, based on the principles in Paterson's essay – or both. (Some of us have varying degrees or types of synaesthesia, too, in which sounds and the shapes of letters, and the different kinds of meanings they combine to express, will be further bound up with, say, colour.)

The meaning in poetry flies higher (despite being, in Ezra Pound's words, 'loaded with ore'[5]; it is packed light, with ore) than the meaning in prose: two sentences with identical meanings can mean vastly different things according to the choice of words and sounds. Sound is made of waves, which produce both noise and a physical effect on the body. These waves make patterns: openness and closedness, assonance and alliteration, rhyme, dissonance, rhythm, even a kind of melody, in cadence. As well as long and short syllables, words have different lengths according to their vowel sounds, use, and positioning in the sentence.

Rhythm is a patterning of relatively regular emphasis, of speed, pauses – which in poetry we call *caesurae* – and of the length of the line itself. We measure the most regular rhythms with metre. Metre is measured in feet of neatly-laid-out syllables, or by the number of syllables that are emphasised in a line. Some irregularity or substitution of the odd foot is permissible, even desirable, but if it gets too irregular it becomes free verse, which may have a defined, if loose, rhythm of its own. But metre by itself is not enough to organise a line, and free verse is not off the hook either.

Every line, every one of these assemblages of vowels, consonants, words, meanings, rhythms and counts and lengths and stresses, with its metaphysical bundle of meanings attached, has a beginning, a middle and an end.

The most problematical part of a line is the end, of course (which leads to the beginning of the next). Many poetry tutors don't like to discuss them at all; there is such a taboo on discussing this most personal aspect of poetry that mentioning it at all feels like crying "Rope!" in the Théatre des Funambules.

The poet Michael Donaghy used to say, "If you write with rhyme it's like walking into the room on stilts or a tightrope, saying, *look what I can do*! But if they can see it coming, you fall on your face and they'll laugh at you instead of admiring your skill." I'd like to add the line ending in general to his analogy.The end stop, the enjambment, the if, and, or but, the clever trick, the effects of rhyme, the carefully-styled hyphen, the repetition, the open ___.

If you use line endings clumsily you run the same risk of falling on your face. Either the reader should glide obliviously over your line ending and straight into the next line, or the jolt should provide some kind of *pleasure* that is inextricable from the *purpose* of the poem.

Pleasure is another concept that might need spelling out here. Poetry exists for pleasure. Like the frisson that must accompany the knowledge of certain death if one falls – imagine how Philippe Petit felt on a good day, say while he was wirewalking between the two towers of Notre Dame Cathedral – one of the chief pleasures afforded by poetry is the stimulation afforded by new combinations of neurons firing in the brain. Sound waves are physical, and brain activity is physical, because energy acts on our tissues: intellectual activity is mixed with sensory, and brings the same kinds of hormonal rewards (euphoria, for example) as physical activity. In his monograph *Wallflowers*, Donaghy wrote about the physical effect on your brain caused by merely mouthing the words while you read.[6]

AS Byatt addressed this issue face-on in the *Cambridge Companion to John Donne*, extracted in the *TLS*:[7]

I came across a remark by a neural network designer about puns. Perhaps, this scientist said, we delight in puns because the neurone connections become very excited by the double input associated with all the stored information for two arbitrarily connected things or ideas. Perhaps we enjoy this excitement. It occurred to me, reading this, that complex metaphors produce infinitely more subtle versions of this excitement and pleasure. I started to think - to use a double entendre that is very pertinent - about the play on words, the play of light on a landscape, the mind at play. I know that this excitement is the primitive thing at the source of why I want to spend my life writing and thinking. I do not have a message to give to the world, I do not wish to seduce or persuade, I want to think as fast as possible, in as complex a way as possible, and put the thinking into verbal forms.

This is the source of the pleasure afforded by Morgan's Hungarian snake, with its progression from one childhood sound-meaning to another, via a playful observation on the Hungarian language, and wrapped up in a sight gag. (Also, note its completeness as a line. It floats complete on the page like one of those floating shelves from IKEA, needing no other visible support.)

In the world of the high wire they call the end points – both ends of the line – the anchor points, and walkers take great care where and how the anchors are to be placed. A line of poetry is no different. The end points need to be placed in such a way that the reader can get from one to the other, and nimbly down to the next, in the way the poet intends.

There are several different kinds of line endings, each carrying its own power, and its own risk of slackness. Blank verse is an elastic form about whose enjambments whole books have been written, which this essay cannot begin to touch. If you've seen wirewalkers jumping or bouncing on their wires, you will know what can be learnt from a form like this: [8]

Best Image of my self and dearer half,
The trouble of thy thoughts this night in sleep
Affects me equally; nor can I like
This uncouth dream, of evil sprung I fear;
Yet evil whence? in thee can harbour none,
Created pure. But know that in the Soule
Are many lesser Faculties that serve
Reason as chief; among these Fansie next
Her office holds; of all external things,
Which the five watchful Senses represent,
She forms Imaginations, Aerie shapes,
Which Reason joyning or disjoyning, frames

All what we affirm or what deny, and call
Our knowledge or opinion; then retires
Into her private Cell when Nature rests.
Oft in her absence mimic Fansie wakes
To imitate her; but misjoyning shapes,
Wilde work produces oft, and most in dreams,
Ill matching words and deeds long past or late.
Some such resemblances methinks I find
Of our last Evenings talk, in this thy dream,
But with addition strange; yet be not sad.

As with the rope, this blank verse of Milton's is coiled of several strands, and cannot be broken without separating those strands. Milton used caesurae to punctuate and create variations of rhythm within the iambic pentameter. This allows him a great freedom

## Milton's blank verse is coiled of several strands

with syntax, which simply serves to strengthen his line further and make it more powerful. His sentences take full advantage, with tumbling images and sub-clauses. If you read from caesura to caesura, you will find that often the 'line within a line' created by the two caesurae is itself a line of iambic pentameter:

among these Fansie next her office holds

frames all what we affirm or what deny

in this thy dream, but with addition strange

Milton was blind when he wrote *Paradise Lost:* he composed each section of 40 lines in his head overnight, and would dictate it to an amanuensis the next day. His family reported that if the secretary were late, he would be pacing up and down, furious, desperate to disgorge himself of the lines he was holding in his head. This metre was formed in the ear.

As well as sound and shape, lines contain intellectual, imagistic and emotional content; there are also a myriad of rhetorical purposes, ego trips and sheer cackhandedness to think about in analysing the line in contemporary verse practice. This essay is not long enough to deal satisfactorily with all these elements, so the list below is more like one of pet peeves – a guide for the unwary – combined with examples of excellence, chosen almost at random from my recent reading. The list runs down a spectrum of enjambment, beginning at the top with full sentences and ending at the bottom with particles so small they might be those .7mm bits of plastic they've discovered in the middle of the Atlantic.

First, there is the completely end-stopped line. This kind of line is rarely found in groups of more than two, but is employed to great effect in Chris Emery's poem, 'Carl's Job'.[9]

> 'We need you to cope with all the little jobs,' smiled Carl.
> 'We want to make sure you target single losers, too,'
> '*Sure,*' I laughed. '*I was very sad to hear about Verna.*'
> 'How the hell do you know about my wife?' asked Carl.
>
> '*I was the one who ran over her that time,*' I replied.
> 'You mean that time at Hennessey's; the time she died?' said
>                                                   Carl.
> '*Right,*' I said. '*The time she died; running off the verge.*'

*She kept her left leg twisting; it was a little strange.'* I smiled.

'What the hell do you want with me?' asked Carl.

*'I've come to apply.'* I said. *'I want to work with you now.'*

The flat tone; length of the lines; the lame extra foot in each line, on top of what would have been roughly iambic pentameter; the presence of further full stops within the lines; the strange reported facial expressions: all work together to show us what the poet calls 'the scariest job interview ever!' The information is declarative, rather than descriptive: the few descriptions are more like something from a police report. There's no room for much else.

Then there is the line that ends on the end of a clause; this is much more common, because more flexible, but it operates in the same way, in units of knowledge. Often two lines make up a sentence, or unit, with a comma or semi-colon at the end of the first one.

In poetry, a unit of knowledge is an image – in Ezra Pound's definition, 'an intellectual and emotional complex in an instant of time.' Pound used this line to construct his pared-back two-liner, 'In a Station of the Metro'. [10] This poem became the 1913 banner around which he rallied the Imagists: 'I wrote a thirty-line poem, and destroyed it because it was what we call work 'of second intensity'. Six months later I made a poem half that length; a year later I made the following *hokku*-like sentence.'

The apparition of these faces in the crowd;
Petals on a wet, black bough.

Today these lines seem almost quaint, with their capital initials, narrative quality and para-rhyme. But Pound was attempting something parallel to what painters at that time were doing: stripping the art down to brass tacks.

When discussing the unit of the line, even a century after Pound's image-poem, it is impossible

## rhyme looms over us like the Post Office Tower in Bloomsbury

to escape from the omnipresence of rhyme. It looms over us like the Post Office Tower in Bloomsbury, so gargantuan that we forget always to see it. Indeed, it is possible for rhyme to creep in where the poet isn't even aware of it. Used well, it has an amazingly galvanising effect on a poem.

Because rhyme is a kind of snapping-shut device for a unit of meaning, it is hard to resist the temptation to deploy the rhyme word at the end of a line. This is what our earliest poetry influences – the nursery thymes – do, and it can lead to a sort of tragic heroic couplet syndrome. Here, from the second stanza of 'The Rape of the Lock' (with spelling modernised):

> Now lapdogs give themselves the rousing shake,
> And sleepless lovers, just at twelve, awake:
> Thrice rung the bell, the slipper knocked the ground,
> And the pressed watch returned a silver sound.
> Belinda still her downy pillow pressed,
> Her guardian sylph prolonged the balmy rest...

This is the tendency that led Oscar Wilde to say, 'There are two ways of disliking poetry. The first way is to dislike it; the other is to read Pope.'

Frederick Seidel employs this device, too. Strangely, in his poetry it gives the impression that the flat-voiced narrator is concealing his feelings, not that he doesn't have any. It creates the same effect of an unreliable narrator as *Catcher in the Rye*, and a poignancy at odds with the poet's rather heartless reputation.[11]

> And when the doctor told me that I could have died.
> And when I climbed up from the subway to the day outside.
> White summer clouds were boiling in the trees.
> I felt like falling to my knees.
> *Stand clear of the closing doors, please! Stand clear of the closing doors,*
> *please!*

This is extreme usage (though note Seidel's internal rhymes, 'boiling' and 'falling' and the repetition of his line-beginning, 'And when').

End-stopped lines are more commonly used to construct the platform onto which a variation springs, in full spangle, to create colour and meaning, backflipping the reader to the next line, with *its* possibilities; or to bring a series of enjambed lines to a conclusion, like a flying trapeze artiste coming to land on the wire at last.

The line that ends on the end of a phrase, rather than a clause, begins to be, in normal usage, the contemporary line: a bit edgy, a bit risky, the judgement of which comes down more to a gut feeling rather than a rule. It will usually be mixed up with lines that break at the end of clauses: an amalgam of enjambment.

Take these two stanzas from near the beginning of Basil Bunting's modernist masterpiece, 'Briggflatts':[12]

> Every birth a crime,
> every sentence life.
> Wiped of mould and mites
> would the ball run true?

No hope of going back.
Hounds falter and stray,
shame deflects the pen.
Love murdered neither bleeds nor stifles
but jogs the draftsman's elbow.
What can he, changed, tell
her, changed, perhaps dead?
Delight dwindles. Blame
stays the same.

Brief words are hard to find,
shapes to carve and discard:
Bloodaxe, king of York,
king of Dublin, king of Orkney.
Take no notice of tears;
letter the stone to stand
over love laid aside lest
insufferable happiness impede
flight to Stainmore,
to trace
lark, mallet,
becks, flocks
and axe knocks.

The thing to notice here is how Bunting, while giving the illusion of 'difficulty', organises his images as neatly as if they were folded in a drawer. The
rhymes don't announce themselves with flashy metre, they simply arrive,
like rocks in a landscape. Nevertheless, each stanza is woven through with
internal rhyme and para-rhyme – elbow/tell her, shame/changed/same,

stray/stays, mites/delight, York/Orkney, Bloodaxe/becks/axe – and each ends on a rhymed couplet. The disintegration of the syntax into a list at the end of the second quoted stanza is not confusing, partly because it is clear *beforehand* what the list is, and partly because it is organised by rhyme, and the logic of the poem.

We can play a game with it, and re-break the lines in the way someone less skilful than Bunting might.

> Every birth a crime, every
> sentence life. Wiped of mould
> and mites, would the ball run
> true? No hope of going back. Hounds
> falter and stray, shame
>             deflects the pen. Love murdered
> neither bleeds nor stifles but jogs
>
> the draftsman's elbow.

What do we see? Orphaned words at the ends of lines, running to catch up with the ones on the line beneath before they get away. Sense harder to get at because of the unsympathetic breaks. Symmetries ruined, and edgy (but empty) rhythms created. 'True', at the start of New Line 4, echoes like the refrain in a '60s pop song. 'Falter and stray, shame' is a line too clotted even to falter, saved only by Bunting's prosody; the penultimate line is now trivial, and the final line portentous and reminiscent of Peter Greenaway. (If we were really going to do the thing properly we would loose it from its moorings and let it drift sadly on its own at the bottom, suddenly carrying on its own the dead weight of everything that has gone before. Oh, wait! There: done.)

After that there is the straightforwardly ambiguous post-modern ending, smack in the middle of a phrase, so that the relationship between the final word and the first one on the line below becomes pivotal for the poem's meaning. This kind of line needs to be crystal clear.

In 'Pour' Philip Gross writes: [13]

> Call it connecting
> one moment with another:
>    water-
>
> in-the-glass with water-in-the-jug,
> two bodies of water
>    and between,
>
> this slick and fluted glitter...

If this isn't 'an intellectual and emotional complex in an instant of time' I don't know what it is; and – notwithstanding its indentations, broken compound, enjambments over stanzas, and lack of verbs – it is held firmly together by the visual imitation of falling water, and the sounds of its water: *connecting, another, water, water, bodies, water,* and the wonderful *glitter*...

There is a tension between the ending of one line and the start of the next. If the second half of an enjambed phrase changes the meaning of the previous line, in a way that doesn't add to the meaning of the poem, it misguides the reader, breaks the anchor point between the two lines and sends the reader flying through the air into the canyon (or water). This can happen if the poet ignores the fact that a word could be read as either a verb or something else: in this case, two words.

So long as alluvial mud remained, and rotted
wood, or rinsed white bones of crocodiles[14]

Did the alluvial mud rot the wood, or rinse the bones of the crocodiles?

In the next example, we must first get past the fact that 'Sat' is being used as an adjective, to describe the state of the grandfather.

Sat on a dining-room chair he had turned
himself years before, he'd sip tea as I played[15]

It's not that 'he' (implied) sat; it's that he *was* sat. Caught out once. Then the verb, 'turned', not only at first suggests a different meaning – that the grandfather had turned *around* in the chair – catching us out twice – but, even as we realise it is 'turned' as in woodworking, acts in the reading as if the next word ('himself') were the object of the transitive form of the verb. Caught out again: three strikes! And into the chasm we drop! There is even a possible reading where it could be said that he had turned the dining room chair *into* himself.

(This couplet also falls prey to a different problem: it has slipped unknowingly, in a poem that is not in metre, into a jaunty dactylic tetrameter. The mood of this metre is at odds with the mood of the poem, and nowhere is this jauntiness or metre repeated.)

There is another model, where the poet takes a figurative expression and breaks it in half. The reader reaches the end of one line, thinks it means one thing, and then discovers a split second later that in fact it means another thing. Done well, this can be a great device in a poem, adding a layer of meaning with economy and wit. Done badly, it means the reader has to go back, reread the first line, realise in advance what it actually is getting at, and then proceed, having gained nothing from the experience. This weakens the poem substantially, renders the poet an unreliable guide, and makes the reader feel – according to his skill and confidence as a reader – either annoyed, or as if the misunderstanding was somehow his fault.

And finally there is the utterly atomised line break, on a preposition or particle, or on a weak word intended to call the very notion of importance into doubt. This is the most dangerous kind of line break, partly because of its difficulty, and partly because of its ubiquity, as so many poets adopt it merely to break up something they think would have looked predictable otherwise, without understanding fully how it works.

Remember Petit's injunction to seek out your materials, get to know them, learn to recognise their properties at a glance? Ending on a preposition or particle creates a particular nervy effect, and operates as part of a system whereby the line is weighted at its first word – so the dying fall of the ending is a ruse, and the first word of the next line picks you up and tautens the whole thing again. In fact, the particle or preposition at the end of the line is what puts the weight on the start of the next line – so you'd better be sure it's really taut enough to sustain the tension this creates.

Highwire artists can write this line, and from the ground below they look as if they're floating. But in reality they are gripping on with toes of pure muscle.

## gripping on with
## toes of pure muscle

Sharon Olds is the exemplar *par excellence* of a nervy, emotional, tense use of this kind of line-break. Putting the stress on the first word of the line below, it creates a sense of urgency as well as hesitancy, and disorients the reader, who then grabs for the emotional content as for a lifeline. In spoken delivery, this line can sound breathy, and lends itself to what we know as the Poetry Voice, full of portentous pauses, intended to alert the listener that something Important (and not normally audible in speech, because in fact based on a typographical construct) is happening. But on the page it races down to the bottom. From 'I Go Back to May 1937': [16]

I see my father strolling out
under the ochre sandstone arch, the
red tiles glinting like bent
plates of blood behind his head, I
see my mother with a few light books at her hip
standing at the pillar made of tiny bricks with the
wrought-iron gate still open behind her, its
sword-tips black in the May air,
they are about to graduate, they are about to get married,
they are kids, they are dumb, all they know is they are
innocent, they would never hurt anybody.
I want to go up to them and say Stop,

Most of the lines here begin big, heavy, emphatic, and seem to lose substance towards the end, tipping the reader onto the next line like rain off the end of a twig – where the same thing happens again. The punctuation (mainly commas) refuses to admit a stop for breath until it's absolutely necessary, so the reader falls like a drop from twig to twig until fairly exhausted. This is an effective technique. On the other hand, aside from the shock and awe of the images – the 'plates of blood', the tortured 'wrought-iron gate' still fruit-lessly open, the 'sword-tips' – it doesn't allow much room for anything else much to be happening in terms of effect. This passage ends with the word the poet wants to say to her young parents: 'Stop' – which is exactly what the reader is not allowed to do.

Marianne Moore, who could not be much more different from Olds ('tight, brisk,/ Neat and hard as an ant'),[17] renders this device deliberate, precise, meditative. She uses it in aid of her (and the reader's) eye, supporting a syllabic scaffolding of gossamer lightness. 'The Mind is an Enchanting Thing' uses the preposition-based line break to direct the traffic of our attention. Rather than trying to be clever with us, she guides us almost as by the hand:[18]

is an enchanted thing
    like the glaze on a
katydid-wing
    subdivided by sun
    till the nettings are legion.
Like Gieseking playing Scarlatti;

like the apteryx-awl
    as a beak, or the
kiwi's rain-shawl
    of haired feathers, the mind
    feeling its way as though blind,
walks along with its eyes on the ground.

This delicacy is achieved by a careful balancing of effects (including, potentially, a high Scrabble score). Line 2 ends on a preposition; in the next stanza, line 3 ends 'without', and in the next, on a new sentence 'It', and in the stanza after that, 'the'. Clearly line 2 in this poem is a place of doubt, or confusion and explanation, of pause before the big leap; where the reader is pointed on towards the main point, the image. But in every stanza lines 1 and 3, and 4 and 5, rhyme. This creates an element of rounding-off, which resolves the question formed by the dangling line-end above.

At the very start of the poem, the mind is enchanting, and then enchanted, 'like the glaze on a' – pause – then the surprise, and the image: 'katydid-wing'. It is the wing we are meant to notice, but the glaze, because we wondered briefly what it was on, retains its shimmering importance. And with that word 'subdivided' the poet shows us how she has made her image work.

The extract by WS Merwin that follows is, characteristically of him, anchored by syntax. There is no punctuation; Merwin's colloquial two-to-three-beat lines keep the poem well moored. This is a style of poetry best written by those who understand sentence construction, who are alert to all the possible meanings of a word.[19]

Why did he promise me
that we would build ourselves
an ark all by ourselves
out in back of the house
on New York Avenue
in Union City New Jersey
to the singing of the streetcar
after the story
of Noah whom nobody
believed about the waters
that would rise over everything

Whether or not this is the kind of poetry that 'floats your boat', this is unquestionably the work of a poet lying down on the wire taking cups of tea. It looks easy, but it takes a great deal of discipline and care to be this simple.

There is a potential spill where he writes, 'that we would build ourselves', which could look like 'ourselves' was the object of 'build'; but the save is immediate: 'an ark all by ourselves'. The first, purely colloquial, iteration becomes an amplifier, characterising the speech of the small boy and symbolising Noah ('whom nobody/ believed') as a child (who has to ask again and again), and thus the child in all of us when dealing with issues of higher importance.

By the same token, the line break on 'after the story/ of Noah whom nobody' might look arbitrary, but it gives the following line anchors for its own full weight: 'believed about the waters.' Does the father believe about the waters? You might well ask.

I recently heard someone say they judged if the lines were working by how they looked on the page. If the poem looks okay, whatever that means, then the lines are working. This statement goes against the entire principle of the line, and what you're up there trying to accomplish. I'm not talking about concrete poetry, or poetry which has been written specifically with a particular shape in mind, like Morgan's snake. Sure, a poem should look nice on the page, but this will change according to the pro- **a poem in a state of** portions of the typeface used, the **organic tensile balance** kerning and general page layout and so on. I think it is more true to say that if a poem works, held together by its own internal tension in a state of organic tensile balance, it will tend to work on the page. The elements of this tension are listed above. Sound – that is, the sound the poem makes, and how it feels in your mouth as you make them – is absolutely critical.

This is the equivalent of understanding the rope's 'soul' – its inner core – just from feeling the outer layer with your fingers. If you really feel the sounds your words make, if you have tuned them as delicately as a violinist tunes his strings, you will never read out your poem 'metrically', with the stresses where they shouldn't fall. "Now IS the WINter Of our DIS-conTENT!" you will not say. In other words, "looking okay" is a *sign, not a condition*, of success.

Philippe Petit's book contains a whole chapter on tricks and exercises which the high-wire walker must learn. These include walking backwards, doing comedy routines, wearing disguises and imitating characters or animals; incorporating other people or animals into the act; 'tricks with a Chinese umbrella or an Indian fan', dancing, jumping, taking tea, lying down. Once he is an accomplished high-wire walker, according to Petit (forgive the masculine), the walker keeps his low wire for practicing these exercises and inventing new ones, making them perfect, discarding the ones that don't work for him.

> Silent and alone, he brings to the high cable everything he has learned down below. He discards the movements space will not support and gathers up the others into a group that he will polish, refine, lighten, and bring closer to himself.

The list of tricks, or exercises, a poet can perform on his or her line is also nearly endless. Some of them are even the same; see the above list and find even one you wouldn't like to see in a poem. 'Limits, traps, impossibilities are nothing to me', writes Philippe Petit. 'Every day I go out to look for them. I believe the whip is necessary only when it is held by the student, not the teacher.' He describes practising in blizzards, in rain, on wobbly lines, in mismatched shoes, in wooden shoes, with people shaking the installation ropes. 'You must struggle against the elements to learn that staying on a wire is nothing ... Limits exist only in the souls of those who do not dream.'

# Notes

[1] The original, much shorter, version of this essay was published by Verse Palace (http://versepalace.wordpress.com), edited by Frances Leviston, in January 2010.

[2] Philippe Petit, trans. Auster, *On the High Wire* (Random House, 1985).

[3] Don Paterson, 'The Lyric Principle', *Poetry Review*, Volumes 97:2 & 97:3 (2007).

[4] Edwin Morgan, 'Siesta of a Hungarian Snake', *Collected Poems 1949-1987* (Carcanet, 1990).

[5] The attribution of this phrase to Pound is not certain.

[6] Michael Donaghy, *Wallflowers* (Poetry Society, 2000).

[7] AS Byatt, 'Observe the neurons: Between, above and below John Donne', *Times Literary Supplement* (September 22, 2006).

[8] John Milton, *Paradise Lost*, Book 5. Adam is responding to Eve's dream, which is a premonition of the temptation by the snake.

[9] Chris Emery, 'Carl's Job', in Roddy Lumsden (ed.), *Identity Parade* (Bloodaxe, 2010).

[10] Ezra Pound, 'In a Station of the Metro', first published in *POETRY* (1913).

[11] 'From Nijinsky's Diary', *Ooga Booga* (Farrar Strauss Giroux, 2006).

[12] Basil Bunting, *Briggflatts* (Faber & Faber, 1965).

[13] Philip Gross, *The Water Table* (Bloodaxe, 2009).

[14] Sinead Morrissey, 'Matter', *Through the Square Window* (Carcanet, 2009).

[15] CL Dallat, 'Grandfather', *The Year of Not Dancing* (Blackstaff Press, 2009).

[16] Sharon Olds, 'I Go Back to May 1937'.

[17] Ted Hughes, 'The Literary Life', *Birthday Letters* (Faber & Faber, 1999).

[18] Marianne Moore, 'The Mind is an Enchanted Thing', Complete Poems (Penguin).

[19] WS Merwin, 'Before the Flood' in *Atlantic Monthly* (September 1998).

Katy Evans-Bush is the author of *Me and the Dead* (Salt, 2008) and *Oscar & Henry* (Rack Press, 2010). She edits the online literary magazine Horizon Review, blogs at Baroque in Hackney, and tutors both independently and for the Poetry School. Her next collection, *Egg Printing Explained*, is due from Salt in Spring 2011.

> katyevansbush.com

Ingram Content Group UK Ltd.
Milton Keynes UK
UKHW011850140323
418559UK00023B/346